Manufactured Homes:
The Buyer's Guide

Manufactured Homes: The Buyer's Guide

How to Realize Your Dream in a Manufactured Home

Steven Taylor

Cycle Publishing / Van der Plas Publications
San Francisco

Published by:
Cycle Publishing
1282 7th Avenue
San Francisco, CA 94122, USA
E-mail: pubrel@cyclepublishing.com
Website: http://www.cyclepublishing.com

Distributed or represented to the book trade by:
USA: Midpoint Trade Books, Kansas City, KS
UK: Orca Books/ Chris Lloyd Sales and Marketing Services, Poole
Australia: Tower Books, Frenchs Forest, NSW

Cover design:
Kent Lytle, Lytle Design, Alameda, CA
Cover photographs courtesy Palm Harbor Homes and Silvercrest Homes

Illustration credits:
Silvercrest Homes: illustrations on pages 9, 12, 23, 26, 39, 104
Palm Harbor Homes: illustrations on pages 2 (frontispiece), 14, 36, 37, 40, 42, 44, 57
Horton Homes: illustrations on pages 38, 39, 41
All other illustrations by the author

Publisher's Cataloging-in-Publication Data
Steven V. Taylor: Manufactured Homes: The Buyer's Guide: How to realize your dream in a manufactured home.
I Title: How to realize your dream in a manufactured home
II. Authorship
Bibliography: p. cm. Includes index.
ISBN 1-892495-42-2, trade paperback edn.; ISBN 1-892495-92-9 (electronic edn.)
1. House buying — manuals and handbooks.
2. Manufactured Housing.
3. Mobile Homes.
Library of Congress Catalog Control Number 20033107274

Manufactured Homes: The Buyer's Guide

How to Realize Your Dream in a Manufactured Home

Steven Taylor

Cycle Publishing / Van der Plas Publications
San Francisco

Published by:
Cycle Publishing
1282 7th Avenue
San Francisco, CA 94122, USA
E-mail: pubrel@cyclepublishing.com
Website: http://www.cyclepublishing.com

Distributed or represented to the book trade by:
USA: Midpoint Trade Books, Kansas City, KS
UK: Orca Books/ Chris Lloyd Sales and Marketing Services, Poole
Australia: Tower Books, Frenchs Forest, NSW

Cover design:
Kent Lytle, Lytle Design, Alameda, CA
Cover photographs courtesy Palm Harbor Homes and Silvercrest Homes

Illustration credits:
Silvercrest Homes: illustrations on pages 9, 12, 23, 26, 39, 104
Palm Harbor Homes: illustrations on pages 2 (frontispiece), 14, 36, 37, 40, 42, 44, 57
Horton Homes: illustrations on pages 38, 39, 41
All other illustrations by the author

Publisher's Cataloging-in-Publication Data
Steven V. Taylor: Manufactured Homes: The Buyer's Guide: How to realize your dream in a manufactured home.
I Title: How to realize your dream in a manufactured home
II. Authorship
Bibliography: p. cm. Includes index.
ISBN 1-892495-42-2, trade paperback edn.; ISBN 1-892495-92-9 (electronic edn.)
1. House buying — manuals and handbooks.
2. Manufactured Housing.
3. Mobile Homes.
Library of Congress Catalog Control Number 20033107274

Special Thanks

I COULD not possibly express how utterly impossible it would have been for me to compile this vast amount of information, as well as some of these great photos, without the incredibly valuable assistance of the following individuals, manufacturers and dealerships:

Woody Bell and Colleen Rogers with Palm Harbor Homes in Texas, who provided me with a large amount of information and numerous photographs and floor plans — far more than anyone else. Nothing got past them without being exceptionally excellent. Colleen's expedience can't be topped.

Craig Flemming with Silvercrest Homes of California, who provided me with photographs and floor plans of some of the most elegant manufactured homes imaginable.

Erik T. Jennifer and the Manufactured Housing Institute, who provided me with whatever lists and statistical information I requested, which were considerable.

Bob Burdin, Robbi Kincaide, and Donna Brewer, of Champion Home of Lugoff, SC, who were a terrific help in acquiring miscellaneous photos and floor plans of new manufactured homes.

Van Woody and Reese Walker, formerly with Luv Homes in Austin, TX, who taught me the right way to sell, finance, set up and service manufactured homes.

My editor, Rob van der Plas, whose guidance and patience led me to understand just what it takes to properly get the message across to the readers, and whose belief in my work sustained this project.

The U.S. Department of Housing and Urban Development for their help both in realizing this project and for their continued support of quality in manufactured housing.

And above all, Laura — my publicist, best friend, and wife. Thanks for all your support.

About the Author

AFTER spending most of his adult life performing, then later producing, within the music and television industries in Hollywood, Nashville, and Austin, Steven Taylor retired from his last position of Record Producer and A&R Director for an independent record label. Still relatively young and looking for new challenges, he decided to conduct a thorough research and write a book that would enlighten the reader about the purchase of some high-ticket item. He found that the only "barely covered" industry was the manufactured housing industry.

After almost three years of in-depth scrutinizing, which included working as a sales rep for a half-dozen dealerships, inspecting factories, attending "insider" seminars, and conducting independent studies, Steven compiled his book *Manufactured Homes: The Buyers Guide*. This book approaches the subject even-handedly, recognizing the needs and problems from both sides of the sales desk.

Steven now resides in Bethune, South Carolina, where he is an independent manufactured housing consultant and spends much of his time as a freelance writer, providing articles on consumer affairs and environmental issues to numerous publications.

Table of Contents

1. Introduction

TODAY, almost one out of every three new homes sold in America is a manufactured home. In fact, in some states, particularly in the South, manufactured homes comprise over half of all new homes currently purchased.

Those single-, double-, triple-, and in some cases even quadruple-wides you have seen moving up and down the highways are quickly becoming the preferred housing alternatives over

Fig. 1.1. Is this a manufactured home? Indeed, it is. (Photo courtesy Silvercrest Homes.)

"money-down-the-rathole" rentals and much more expensive site-built homes.

A manufactured home can cost you less than half that of a comparable standard site-built house and, because site-built homes are taxed as real estate and manufactured homes (when financed separately from the land) can be taxed as personal property, you can save additional money come tax time. Many of today's manufactured homes are able to withstand winds over 100 miles per hour. These sturdy structures have superior insulation, are dimensionally exact and cost practically nothing to maintain.

A properly appointed multi-section manufactured home can easily be mistaken for a high dollar site-built house, plus manufactured homes are far less likely to catch on fire than conventional houses.

Is there a down side to all this? You bet there is!

At the time of purchase, a bad decision on your part can cost you thousands of dollars or even prevent you from buying one of these homes at all. If you don't negotiate your contracts properly you can become a victim of down payment or service misunderstandings, which can easily negate any previous "bargains" you may have worked really hard to achieve. Lending practices have grown so out of control in some regions, that literally one out of every five manufactured homes ends up being repossessed. Although all manufactured homes must pass strict HUD requirements, there can be a significant difference in the quality of construction from one home to another. Only a properly informed and wary buyer can be certain to avoid these oversights.

The average manufactured home shopper is ill-equipped to determine the material, feature or construction qualities of these homes. Plus, a small (but swiftly diminishing) number of dealerships sometimes practice ultra-high pressure and less-than-honest sales tactics, which are aimed at misleading buyers into spending more money to get less house and after-sale servicing than they would receive had they been better informed and prepared. Although the vast majority of manufactured home sales professionals are well-intentioned and eager to give you sincere advice and service, every now and then a "bad apple" can appear.

I have spent the last few years researching this gigantic industry as one of them. I thoroughly explored their factories, read many of their books, attended their seminars and shopped at numerous sales lots. I took up employment with various dealerships so I could understand exactly how they work and where their priorities lie (sort of an "earn while you learn" situation). During this time I spec'd out, ordered and sold a large number of manufactured homes, from older single-wide trade-ins to some amazingly elegant double and triple-wides, some with log-like siding, state-of-the-art everything, huge decks and steeply pitched roofs. I placed these homes in areas ranging from low-rent mobile home parks to picturesque estates. Plus, I arranged all of their financing and service. Throughout this experiment I couldn't help but notice the huge gap between truly good and bad dealerships that exist out there. With a little bit of insight, these "good guys" will become fairly easy for you to recognize. Essentially, you will be undertaking a "truth seeking" mission. Although this gigantic industry has been accused of being somewhat of a "den of thieves," you should understand that for every dishonest salesperson you may confront, there are hundreds of hard working, professional manufactured home consultants who will gladly help you find and purchase an excellent home. There are crooks in every walk of life. Don't allow this unfair reputation to deter you from buying one of these marvelous homes. When I first undertook this endeavor, I had every intention of exposing what I mistook to be a sinister group of hoodlums within a horrific industry. I thought that the average manufactured home shopper was in for a treacherous ride. I was wrong.

Although, like in the automobile industry, the stereotypical dishonest sales person was considered to be the norm, in truth I very seldom came across one of those wretched characters. I'm not saying they're not out there. I dealt with a few of them. I even assisted in the prosecution of a dealership that was engaged in fraud on a wide scale. I believe that within the next few years these fly-by-night dealerships will virtually cease to exist.

As I worked at each of these dealerships, hardly a day passed that shoppers would arrive with arms crossed, wives clutching their purses to their chests, the scared words "just looking" coming from their mouths and numerous other gestures of obvious fear and mistrust. Maybe a few of them were afraid for a reason, but I would imagine most of them simply had held the typical stereotype of an untrustworthy sales person. Many were blatantly dishonest with me, probably fearing that if I knew how much they could afford (or couldn't), then I would somehow take advantage of them. Hopefully, some light will be shed on the true nature of these professionals by the time you've finished this book. Some of the finest individuals I've known make their living in the manufactured housing business.

This book will guide you through the history of this young industry, as well as provide a reality check on facts vs. myths. You will take a tour through the complete construction process, from the ground pad all the way up through the tip of the roof, so you'll know exactly what to look for and what to ask your salesperson.

I'll point out some of your financial options so you can better choose which home is best suited for your particular cash flow and credit situation, and give you a general idea as to how these lenders operate. Plus, you'll learn a few tricks to assist you in negotiating a fair price.

Fig. 1.2. Luxurious comfort at an affordable price. (Photo courtesy Silvercrest Homes.)

Once your home has been set up on your property, the sky's the limit on how you can improve and customize your manufactured home. This book will provide you with several ideas on how to create a living environment that is perfectly suited for your wants and needs.

It may at first seem simple enough to just follow the worksheets and attempt to buy your home without first reading this entire book. Don't take this short-cut! The *Do First Checklist*, *Client Introduction Sheet*, *Apples To Apples*, and *Setup Checklist* won't be nearly as effective unless you fully understand how to use them properly. This book was written to educate you and the help sheets were designed to guide you through the entire shopping/buying process.

You should have a wonderful time shopping for, purchasing and living in the home of your dreams. Spending the necessary time reading this material can result in a lifetime of happiness in your home. Don't depend upon luck but put yourself in control and come out a winner.

2.

The History of Manufactured Homes

IMAGINE, say a few thousand years ago, one of the first non-human-powered vehicles—an ox-cart or something similar, and the proud owner, and no doubt manufacturer, was not able to reach his abode in the darkness of night. He most likely, in order to stay off the critter-infested ground, made his bed in his cart. Voila! This unknown soul just invented the first "trailer home."

As nomadic notions affected the inhabitants of our planet, more and more people were utilizing their carts and wagons as occasional nighttime sleeping facilities. Try to imagine gypsies with-

Fig. 2.1. Today's manufactured home is the outcome of many years of development and improvement of the basic "trailer home" concept. (Photo courtesy Palm Harbor Homes.)

out their ornate wagons, or American pioneers without the vaunted Conestoga wagons of our nation's rich past. That would be impossible, wouldn't it?

Centuries passed with no actual documentation (to our knowledge) pertaining to the construction of a manufactured home until 1764, when a company out of London, England shipped a two-story panelized structure to the town of Cape Ann, MA.

By the turn of the 20th Century, the British were building primitive custom vans with provisions for sleeping and lounging. These were terribly uncomfortable and ungainly, but incredibly "in vogue" within certain groups of the upper class.

During this same decade, an unknown American is said to have devised a fifth-wheel hitch attachment for the towing of a travel wagon he'd either constructed or re-implemented. This led to a few self-appointed inventors constructing covered trailers and converting long automobiles into vehicles that could accommodate some sort of sleepover. At this point, though, none had been mass-produced.

In 1926, a small New York manufacturing firm began mass-producing mobile homes for vacation use. These were fundamentally sleepers with tiny dining areas and no plumbing, but were much coveted by many "modern" Americans, who were joining a growing crowd of family campers. These contrivances were popularly known as "trailer coaches" and were soon available nationwide. It was definitely an attractive alternative to sleeping and dining on the dirt.

The onset of World War II greatly accelerated the production of "trailer coaches," creating competition among the existing manufacturers and opening the doors for many more. Factory workers could move themselves and their families from one location to another with little expense. Needing more living space, some of these trailers were as much as 30 feet or more in length. Rudimentary plumbing was being installed, allowing for small bathrooms and functioning kitchens, along with simple electrical hookups and gas lines.

By the end of World War II, many families were using these "trailer coaches" as permanent homes, oftentimes placing them on more solid foundations and customizing them to suit their living needs. By the late 50s and early 60s, many enterprising land owners implemented trailer hookups and operated those famous/infamous "trailer parks."

You may remember a 1960s Lucille Ball movie, "The Long, Long Trailer." Although portrayed as a travel trailer, that shiny towable was actually a "Blue Moon" mobile home, which was designed, more or less, for permanent placement in a mobile home park.

As the demand for these penny-wise abodes grew, so did their dimensions. The original "trailer coaches" were almost always 8 feet in width. By the 1940s one could be found (rarely) 10 feet in width. By the 1960s 12-foot widths were available to buyers, and the first two-section homes were introduced to the public. These are commonly referred to as double-wides, which are simply two towable structures which are placed together, side-by-side, creating a much larger structure which is much more square and "house-like" than a standard mobile home, also known as a single-wide.

Double-wides don't have siding on their marriage walls, so when these sections are properly joined together, or "married,"

Fig. 2.2. Yes, in the early days, they really looked like trailers: Late 50s 2-bedroom single-wide.

one could hardly tell that this originated as two separate structures.

Building Them Safer and Better

Double-wides so dramatically revolutionized the manufactured housing industry and were purchased by so many families that, by the 1970s, one mobile home was built for every three site-built homes. With growth comes pain, and this burgeoning industry produced homes of immensely varying levels of quality. Many of these homes were built with flimsy 2 in. x 2 in.* studs in their exterior walls, 24 in. apart and barely stout enough for a large adult to lean against without falling through. There could be very little insulation, rickety plumbing, treacherous floors and roofs too weak to walk on. Warranties were non-existent and manufacturers, as well as dealerships, constantly went out of business. There was very little enforceable regulation. The numerous regional associations worked extremely hard to police the industry and had made tremendous headway for the industry, but they lacked the ability to enforce their standards. Thus, in 1974, Congress had the U.S.

---

* Throughout this book, feet and inches will be represented by the abbreviations ft. and in. respectively

Fig. 2.3. Double-wide from the early 1970s.

Department of Housing and Urban Development devise a national building code known as the National Mobile Home Construction and Safety Standards Act (42 USC), also known as the HUD Code. Manufactured homes had the distinction of being the only form of private and single-family structures subject to federal regulation. This legislation became effective in June of 1976.

The Housing Act of 1980 further enhanced the industry's standing by defining mobile homes as buildings, rather than vehicles. This legislation directed that all mobile homes produced since 1976 were to be referred to as "manufactured homes" in all federal laws and literature. This legislation also outlined the standards for Wind Zone requirements (to ensure the home is adequately rigid to withstand the wind forces encountered in the region where the home is to be placed) and for U_0 values, which are the coefficient of heat transmission, in order to maintain the home at 70 degrees F with a specified BTU output by the heating unit (BTU, which stands for British Thermal Unit, is the standardized measure of heat output). They are divided into Thermal Zones I, II and III, depending on the prevailing climate in the re-

HUD's Manufactured Home Construction Standards

Manufactured homes are built as dwelling units of at least 320 square feet in size with a permanent chassis to assure the initial and continued transportability of the home.

All transportable sections of manufactured homes built in the U.S. after July 15, 1976, must contain a red label. The label is the manufacturer's certification that the home section is built in accordance with HUD's construction and safety standards. HUD standards cover Body and Frame Requirements, Thermal Protection, Plumbing, Electrical, Fire Safety and other aspects of the home. They are published in the Code of Federal Regulations at 24 CFR 3280.

gion where they are to be placed. Snow load capacities for roofs are also specified according to the region where the manufactured home is to be placed. Wind zones are divided into Wind Zones I, II, and III. You can contact your state MHI (Manufactured Housing Institute, see Appendix A for addresses) to find out in exactly which areas you would be setting your home, or you may contact HUD by calling toll free: 1-800-767-7468 or by contacting their web-site at http://www.hud.gov.

During the 1980s the growing dimensions of the industry were proportionally matched by the dimensions of the manufactured homes themselves. The classic single-wides had been expanded in width to 14, and sometimes even 16 feet. Some were being built to lengths of 70 feet. Not needing the complicated and more expensive setup procedure required by a double-wide, new homeowners were able to enjoy additional square footage without devastating their budgets. Current single-wides can be up to 80 feet long and 16 to18 feet wide. Also, single-wides allow for smaller lots and setup areas. In the past, single-wides were quite easy to finance, as they could be easily towed away by the repo man. More on that later.

Fig. 2.4. Notice the tail-lights affixed to this older single-wide—à la pre-Housing Act of 1980.

Throughout the 80s and 90s the manufactured housing revolution built up steam and expanded enormously at a rapid rate. Set up side-by-side, countless dealerships lined highways on the outskirts of many cities, particularly in the south and southwest. There were hard-working mom and pop stores, big name manufacturers and a few of those "fly-by-night" monsters that led to some terribly unfair perceptions of the industry as a whole by many consumers. Fortunately, due to timely legislation, diligent marketing by caring manufacturers and a better informed public, these "bad apples" started going "belly-up" and have, for the most part, ceased to exist. This infant industry has taken the initiative to police itself in a way which can only improve on the quality of its products and enhance the image of manufactured homes. In fact, ever since the mid 1930s numerous manufacturers and associations have been striving to improve upon the industry and its products.

One organization that sticks out as truly fair, conscionable and immensely effective is the Manufactured Housing Institute, or MHI. Its mission statement is to represent all segments of the manufactured housing industry. MHI serves its members by providing research, promotion, education and government relations

Fig. 2.5 A typical 1980s double-wide.

programs, and by building consensus within the industry. This organization stridently pushed the Manufactured Housing Improvement Act of 2000 and is now working to implement its provisions and requirements, such as updating the HUD Code standards on a timely basis, clarifying the scope of federal preemption, and providing HUD staff with additional resources to run the federal program for manufactured housing. Here is a brief history of the Manufactured Housing Institute, as provided by Al Hesselbart, Vice President of the Manufactured Housing Heritage Foundation:

> The current MHI organization came into being on September 1, 1975 following about ten years of negotiations between the major associations representing manufacturers, dealers, suppliers, and state organizations.
>
> Trailer Coach Association (TCA) formed March 5, 1936, and headquartered in Los Angeles, CA., represented the industry in the western portion of the country. TCA held its first show in Los Angeles in May 1936. TCA founded "Trailer Life" magazine as its house organ and promotional periodical in 1941. The magazine was sold to Art Rouse in 1958. The TCA developed a set of construction standards in 1951, which were optional to their members. TCA's headquarters be-

Fig. 2.6. Another 1980s double-wide, looking rather utilitarian with those tiny windows.

came the offices of MHI Western Region.

Mobile Home Manufacturers Association (MHMA) formed in August, 1936, as the Trailer Coach Manufacturers Association, and headquartered first in Detroit and then moved to Chicago in 1938, represented the industry in the Midwest and East. Seeds of this organization were first planted at the Tin Can Tourists convention at Grand Rapids, MI. in 1935. MHMA held its first show in August 1939, at Manistee, MI. Twenty-eight manufacturers showed 95 models. The MHMA developed a set of standards for mechanical and material components in 1958. The national headquarters was moved to Chantilly, VA in 1972, and to Washington D.C. in 1974. MHMA's offices became MHI national headquarters.

The Mobile Home Craftsman's Guild was a group of manufacturers, all MHMA members, who joined together in 1958 to develop the "Gold Seal" program as a pledge to follow the latest standards for mechanical, material, and design components. In 1964, The TCA standards and the MHMA standards were combined under the auspices of the American National Standards Institute in 1964, with the ANSI program still in use. Following this combination, the Gold Seal lost much of its effectiveness and was no longer in use in 1975.

The South East Mobile Home Institute (SEMHI) was formed in 1967. It represented the interests of state manufactured housing associations in the states of North and South Carolina, Georgia, Florida, Alabama, Mississippi, Virginia, Kentucky, Tennessee and West Virginia. The association continued to exist as a representative of its member state organizations following the creation of MHI, but after one to two years it was felt it was redundant and disbanded.

Mobilehome Dealers National Association (MDNA) represented the retailers nationally and was not directly involved in the forming of MHI but did cease to exist at the same time as SEMHI.

The Board of MHMA approved the formation of MHI at its annual meeting in March of 1975, TCA's board approved it on June 1, 1975, and SEMHI approved it on September 1, 1975, making the creation of MHI officially accepted by all participating bodies.

This team of industry leaders with the support of many others working on task forces and committees shaped the future of MHI. By merging the finest attributes of all of the various associations, they created an organization which politically represented the industry nationally before lawmaking bodies. By standardizing methods, quality and safety of manufacturing materials and techniques they lead the way for the growth of today's manufactured home industry.

As state associations gained strength and represented the local community operators and retailers to state legislative bodies and provided shows, and other marketing activities for their membership, The National Manufactured Housing Federation was formed in 1977 under the leadership of Holt Blomgren and others to facilitate development of a national consensus on key issues. Blomgren, Executive Director of the Indiana Manufactured Housing Association, became its first Executive Director and Paul Stiner its first president. Originally involving seven state associations (California, Illinois, Indiana, Michigan, Ohio, Texas and Washington), the federation grew to represent 41 states by 1983. The Iowa MHI was the first association to join with the original seven.

In March of 1991, at the Nashville Manufactured Housing Show, the Executive Committees of MHI and the Federation agreed to pursue a merger. In September, the Board of the Federation approved the action at its meeting in Las Vegas and the MHI Board approved the merger at its meeting in October in San Diego. The National Manufactured Housing Federation thus became the Federated States Division of MHI in October, 1991. This action effectively joined all aspects of the manufactured housing industry—suppliers, manufacturers, retailers and communities, into one associated body.

In 1985, Danny Ghorbani, a former MHI Executive, formed an organization to champion the rights and interests of housing manufacturers under the National Manufactured Housing Construction and Safety Standards Act of 1974 (HUD Code). The organization originally known as the Association for Regulatory Reform (ARR) added Manufactured Housing to its name in 1997 to become MHARR and clarify its purpose of representing the manufactured housing industry interests. While not directly related to MHI, MHARR has similar interests and does work cooperatively with MHI on legislative issues.

Fig. 2.7. Elegant modern triple-wide. (Photo courtesy Silvercrest Homes)

The Manufactured Housing Institute, along with the numerous state manufactured housing institutes, have been extremely effective at leveling the playing field and at eliminating the few remaining "ne'er-do-wells" within the industry. With the advent of urban sprawl, countless prospective homeowners have taken into consideration purchasing manufactured homes, when only a few years ago they would have scoffed at the idea of ever owning one of those "trailer houses."

In order to provide larger and more elegant housing for these newly interested potential buyers, the manufacturers designed and built larger double-wides and added features such as upgraded appliances, taped and textured walls, hand textured ceilings with elegant moldings, top-of-the-line windows and siding materials, and many other amenities that improved the functional, structural and aesthetic value of these homes.

The demand for larger and more permanent looking structures brought on the triple-wide, which is fundamentally a double-wide, plus an additional smaller unit which attaches to either the front or the rear of the structure. Additionally, many manufactured home owners add on site-built garages or other structures… more about that, later.

Just recently, primarily on the west coast, some innovative manufacturers have been producing quadruple-wides, many of which actually have a second story as well as contracted site-built additions included with their initial purchase.

3. How Good Are Manufactured Homes?

THERE are a number of misconceptions still floating around about perceived inadequacies of manufactured homes as compared to conventionally built ones. In this chapter, we will take a look at those.

• Myth:

It is commonly perceived that manufactured homes are more vulnerable to fires than other single-family structures.

• Reality:

According to an annual report released by the Oklahoma State Fire Marshall's Office, manufactured homes, as structures, are no more prone to catching fire than site-built homes. In fact, according to the Foremost Insurance Company, site-built homes are more than twice as likely to experience fires than manufactured homes. They state that 17 out of every 1,000 site-built homes catch fire, as opposed to only 8 per 1,000 manufactured homes. These studies also indicated that post-HUD manufactured homes burn less often than pre-HUD manufactured homes. As quoted by Richard Wettergreen, Assistant Vice President for Marketing Communications and Research at Foremost Insurance Company:

Manufactured homes are the only homes with a national building code. The fire study indicates that HUD standards, adopted in 1976, have a positive effect on fire safety in manufactured housing.

When construction methods and standards are considered, it appears to be a distinct and safe advantage to live in a factory-built home. It's time the myth of high fire potential in manufactured housing is laid to rest once and for all.

In accordance with the HUD Code, strict standards require flame spread (a measure of how fast a fire spreads once started) and smoke generation (a measure of how much smoke is caused in case of fire) in materials, egress (i.e. escape) windows in all bedrooms, smoke detectors, and at least two exterior doors, which must be remote from each other and reachable via only unlockable doors. All other types of structure are required only to have one exterior door and no "reachability" requirement.

• Myth:

Manufactured homes are fundamentally "tornado magnets."

Fig. 3.1. Two-story quadruple wide. (Photo courtesy Silvercrest Homes.)

• Reality:

On July 13th, 1994, HUD issued revisions to the previous wind safety provisions of the HUD Code. This was brought about by the assessment of the immense damage and destruction caused by Hurricane Andrew, which struck the southern tip of Florida and the Gulf Coast regions of Louisiana back in August, 1992, with horrendous winds in excess of 150 miles-per-hour.

In accordance to HUD's new Basic Wind Zone Map, the wind safety standards in areas prone to hurricane–force winds (known as Wind Zones II and III), the wind safety standards require that manufactured homes be resistant to winds up to 100 miles per hour in Wind Zone II and 110 miles-per-hour in Wind Zone III. The standard for manufactured homes in both of these zones is now far more stringent than the current regional and national building codes for site-built homes within these same wind zones.

Each state has its own regulatory standards as to how manufactured homes are installed and anchored. It must be understood that only by properly installing and anchoring one of these structures, can the wind resistance standards be realized by the manufactured home owner. As a required part of the storm protection provisions of the HUD Code, for each manufactured home sold, the manufacturer must include installation instructions to properly support and anchor the home.

There has never been one bit of scientific or meteorological evidence to suggest that manufactured structures attract lightning or high winds, including tornadoes. The reality is that the older "mobile home" parks were fundamentally placed in rural settings or on the outskirts of municipalities, which have a tendency to be in paths of lesser resistance for damaging winds or storms, which would be passing through. Newer manufactured homes are also much more prevalent in rural settings. Thus, they too are naturally in areas which may be more open and vulnerable to severe weather situations.

In areas designated as Wind Zone I, manufactured homes, when properly installed and anchored, must be able to withstand sustained wind forces of up to 70 miles-per-hour. However, well-installed manufactured homes in these areas can normally withstand much higher winds without sustaining any appreciable damage.

In all truth, a direct hit from a tornado will destroy practically any structure. An F-4 or F-5 tornado will completely destroy even the strongest building. An F-5 will actually peel the road pavement off the ground, leaving just dirt. In the event of a tornado, there are only two choices: Drive away from the area as quickly as possibly, making sure to travel *away* from the storm, or locate a covered underground shelter. A ditch or culvert is the last resort as a tornado can simply suck you from your position.

• Myth:

Manufactured homes do not retain their value as well as site-built homes.

• Reality:

That common viewpoint is completely false. In truth, manufactured homes are directly on par with site-built homes when it comes to depreciation. Homes, regardless of type, which are set up in bad neighborhoods and areas with lower real estate values, will depreciate in spite of the condition of the structure on that property. If a manufactured home is set up on a permanent foundation, and if, in the case of a multi-section structure, the sections are properly married, the ground pad drains properly, and the whole building is strongly anchored, the longevity of this home is equal to that of any similar site-built house. To this advantage, add the fact that the cost of the manufactured home is significantly lower than that of the site-built home, and you'll see the manufactured home buyer will enjoy instant appreciation between what the home actually costs and what its market value has quickly become. In many cases, a multi-section manufactured home has sold for more the second time than the first. A properly set up and maintained manufactured home can truly be a fantastic investment.

• Myth:

Manufactured homes are not as well built as site built homes.

• Reality:

Both site-built and manufactured homes are constructed with the same materials, including windows, doors, roof trusses and shingles, siding, flooring, and most other components. In fact, many manufactured homes utilize 2 x 6 exterior wall studs, instead of the standard 2 x 4 studs almost always used in the construction of site-built homes.

Also, many have steel straps holding the walls to the floors and the roof to the walls, so the strength of the entire structure is superior to that of an average site-built house. Required plumbing is usually CPVC, which is generally considered the superior material for fresh, gray or black water at any temperature without breaking down like polybutylene or standard PVC (polyvinyl chloride).

When you look through one of these homes you will notice that the gaps between the floor and the bottom of the interior doors seem to be abnormally large. HUD requires each manufactured home to "breathe" properly. The cooler air must flow from room to room over the floor, as the warmer air does the same just below the

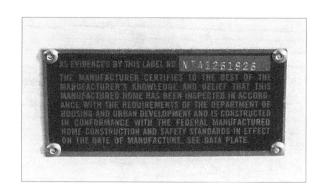

Photo 3.2. Example of the HUD tag that gets affixed to every manufactured home.

ceiling through vents over the doors (primarily bedroom doors). This provides for a much more proper air exchange, which equalizes the temperature and provides a greater volume of fresh air throughout the house. Very few site-built homes utilize this method.

All manufactured homes are built on jigs (platforms), which are dimensionally exact. Thus, every manufactured home is perfectly plumb when it leaves the factory.

Unlike site-built homes, manufactured houses also have to be built to the stringent HUD Code standards. Built in a controlled, factory environment, manufactured homes are tested and inspected by HUD for construction, strength and durability, design, fire resistance, energy efficiency and performance of internal systems.

HUD inspectors thoroughly inspect each and every home at every single factory. Not a single home leaves the factory without a red HUD tag affixed to the rear of the building, which certifies that the home has past HUD's rigid standards. These tags can *only* be attached by a HUD inspector.

• Myth:

Manufactured homes look like trailers.

Fig. 3.3. Does this look like a trailer? Two-story manufactured home. (Photo courtesy Silvercrest Homes.)

• Reality:

Obviously, quite a few people know better than that. But not everyone has been enlightened as to the tremendous progress made by this industry over the past two decades. With floor plans ranging from a few hundred square feet to over three thousand square feet, and models such as ranch styles, Cape Cods, California bungalows, split logs, and Mediterranean style with stucco walls and tiled roofs, as well as an ever-growing assortment of two storied beauties, these old-fashioned concepts will die with all other groundless myths.

4. The Way They Are Built

I N THIS chapter, you'll find a detailed rundown on the construction of a typical manufactured home.

The T-Frame

Every manufactured home (or each section, in the case of multi-section homes) is built on top of a metal "T-Frame," which is made up of steel I-profile beams (i.e. a steel beam with a cross-section that resembles the shape of the letter "I"). Once installed on your home site, it will be the metal frame that is supported on top of the foundation.

Fig. 4.1. The T-frame, the "foundation" of any manufactured home. (Photo courtesy Palm Harbor Homes.)

There are two basic types of I-beams. The most common is composed of corrugated steel, which is rippled (like a corrugated cardboard box and is manufactured in Asia. The other type is made of smooth steel of a greater thickness, and are made in America. Because the latter are heavier and stronger (but also more expensive) the American I-beams are preferable, although the Asian I-beams are quite adequate under most circumstances. At the front of each T-frame is a hitch, which connects it to the hauler during transport to the site. Some are welded on and therefore troublesome to remove (they call unwanted attention to your home as being a "trailer home"). Higher quality homes have removable hitches, which can be stored underneath the home out of sight.

Figs. 4.2 and 4.3. US steel I-beam (top) and corrugated Asian I-beam (bottom)

33

Flooring

Attached to the top of the I-beams are floor joists. A majority of manufacturers use pressure treated 2 in. x 6 in. pine boards running the width of the frame. Some homes (usually high end single-wides) use 2 in. x 8 in. joists, while low-end homes use 2 in. x 4 in. joists. Another manufacturing shortcut is to run joists length-wise, butt-lapping them together at intervals. Stay away from homes built this way as serious structural problems are almost certain to occur. This category was intentionally left off the *Apples To Apples* sheets since you should not consider a home built this poorly. Most floor joists are placed 16 in. on center (OC). This is far more desirable than placing them 24 in. OC.

Running the perimeter of this sub-flooring are bands, which are the same materials as the joists. Since the floors are wider than the frames, they hang out beyond the width of the I-beams. Most manufactured homes have steel outriggers attached to the sides of the I-beams to support the weight of the extended floors. However, many do not extend all the way out to the outer edge, so be sure to look underneath your prospective new home to make certain that these outriggers extend all the way out to the outer walls. This is the only way they can sufficiently support their weight. If they don't, you are probably looking at future uneven settling of the walls and separation from the roof. This condition is called "crowning" and will most likely happen after just a few years (like after your warranty has just expired). Crowning creates roof, ceiling and duct leaks, which in turn can cause windows and doors to jam and walls and ceilings to crack. You can save yourself a whole lot of trouble in the future by making sure that the outriggers reach all the way.

Nestled underneath the sub-flooring is a blanket of insulation. It's ability to keep out heat and cold is determined by what is called the R (resistance) factor. The higher the R-factor, the better it insulates. HUD requires minimum R-factors of 4 for floors, 4 for walls, and 7 for ceilings. When ordering your home, you should upgrade the insulation to higher R-factors: Typical homes have R factors of 14/11/19, making the home much more comfortable and cheaper to heat or cool.

When the insulation is being attached to the underside of the floor joists, the AC/heating ductwork and plumbing are also installed. The entire floor is flipped upside-down to do this work more efficiently.

Plastic sheeting is attached to the underside, keeping out moisture and critters. Different manufacturers use different materials, so don't neglect to inspect this important area.

Countless sales pitches have been contrived to promote one type of floor decking over another kind (or brand). By far the most commonly installed floor decking is particle-board. Although it may be referred to as "Novadek," "Novoflor" or some other variation, it's still particle board, a product made up of sawdust mixed with tree resins, pressed into sheets under pressure. Particle-board is the densest and hardest floor decking material pres-

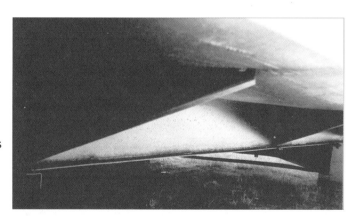

Fig. 4.4. Notice these outriggers do not reach the outer portion of the structure.

Fig. 4.5. These outriggers are within 3 inches of the end—much better.

ently used on a large scale. It is dimensionally exact and can be formed into extremely large sheets (the other materials are always 4 ft. x 8 ft.). This makes for a more attractive floor when covered with vinyl, as it reveals fewer seams. It also doesn't "creak" like some plywood and is quite inexpensive to replace. Kept dry, particle-board is a superior flooring material which is good for the life of any home. There is only one potential drawback with this material. Remaining wet for only a few days, particle board expands and disintegrates. Because of this, many buyers tend to consider other floor decking options.

Plywood floors are available options with most manufacturers and standard with a few others. The material is widely available, holds nails extremely well, and stands up fairly well to water. Although plywood can delaminate if it remains wet for too long, it won't disintegrate and would require a long period of time to rot through. If you choose plywood flooring, be sure it's ¾ in. tongue in groove. Thinner plywood, whether ⅜ in.., ½ in., or ⅝ in. thick, will flex and bow, creating numerous flooring problems within just a few years.

The newest floor-decking product on the market is oriented strand board (OSB). OSB consists of wood chips (not to be con-

Fig. 4.6. Laying down insulation. (Photo courtesy Palm Harbor Homes.)

fused with old fashioned "chip board"), which are aligned in varying directions, mixed with waterproof marine adhesives and then compressed under extreme pressure. Like particle-board, it is extremely dense and hard. However, unlike particle-board, OSB is essentially waterproof and doesn't tend to chip off into chunks. It usually costs less than plywood and is fast becoming very popular not only as a great floor decking choice, but also for wall sheathing and roof decking. As a testament to OSB's resistance to water, many boat manufacturers use it for decking on their boats.

There really isn't a bad choice for floor decking, but since no wood product is completely impervious to water, the best advice is to protect all floors from wetness by properly maintaining all plumbing connections and moisture barriers. If you do this, your flooring should last throughout the life of your home regardless of which decking material was used.

After the sub-floor insulation is attached, the floor decking is stapled on top of the joists. This decking is OSB. Next, vinyl floor

Fig. 4.7. Installation of OSB flooring. (Photo courtesy Palm Harbor Homes.)

covering is installed, but not carpeting.

Walls

When your friendly salesperson is "feature/benefitting" your prospective home, she/he will almost invariably mention that the exterior walls are constructed with 2 in. x 4 in. studs, 16 in. OC. I say "invariably" because 2 in. x 4 in. studs, 16 in. OC are standard on virtually all manufactured homes being built today. Some are still built with weaker 2 in. x 3 in. studs or are 24 in. OC (on center). Fortunately, structures this inferior are extremely rare these days.

You can normally upgrade the exterior wall studs to 2 in. x 6 in., 16 in. OC. This is always good to do if ordering your home and if it fits into your budget, as it upgrades your exterior walls' maximum insulation from R11 to R19. Lower utility bills will completely cover the extra cost within just a few years, outside noises will be deadened and your house will be much sturdier. These walls are required if you are placing your home in colder regions (known as Thermal Zones II and III).

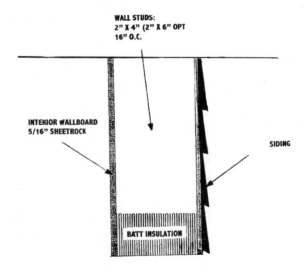

Fig. 4.8. Typical sidewall construction detail. (Illustration courtesy Horton Homes.)

Many manufacturers further strengthen their wall attachments by stapling steel straps from the lower portion of the exterior wall studs to the sub-floor bands and from the upper portion of the exterior wall studs to the base of the roof. These add a tremendous amount of wind resistance and overall strength to a house. They are required in all salt water coastal counties and certain other locations, which are subject to naturally occurring high winds (These areas are called wind zones II and III).

Next, all interior and exterior walls are attached.

Almost all interior walls are built with 2 in. x 3 in. studs, 24 in. OC. There's nothing really wrong with utilizing skinnier and weaker walls on the interior sections because they don't bear any structural weight and they're a whole lot cheaper to build. What many homeowners may *not* enjoy is that there is very little sound blockage from room to room unless these interior walls are insulated, which is hardly ever an option. The ideal interior walls are constructed with 2 in. x 4 in. studs, 16 in. OC and insulated with R 11 fiberglass batts. These walls are extremely solid and more sound resistant. On top of that, even hanging pictures is a more pleasant experience since the studs are closer together and easier

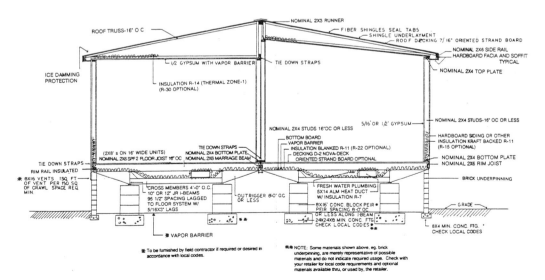

Fig. 4.9. Typical double-wide cross-section illustration. (Illustration courtesy Horton Homes.)

to locate. Expect this to only be an option on the most opulent manufactured homes.

Be sure to ask your salesperson if the electrical outlet boxes are attached directly to the studs and if striker plates are placed in front of the wall wiring routes. A surprising number of manufacturers neglect to do these simple things in order to cut corners. What you don't see can hurt you. Pulling the plug from an outlet attached only to the sheetrock can put a large hole in the wall, and inserting a nail or screw into an electrical wire can electrocute you. This truly does happen.

HUD requires all manufactured home interior wall panels to be comprised of gypsum sheetrock (in some areas known as drywall). This material is fire retardant and can come in thicknesses of $3/8$ in., $1/2$ in. and $5/8$ in.. The thicker it is, the more it deadens sound. You should note that these walls are generally covered with vinyl wall-papering and are very easy to keep clean.

Those 1-inch strips running down the walls every 4 feet (they're called battens) don't appear very attractive to some buyers, but to most they're just fine. Battens cover the seams between the drywall sheets and allow the walls to bend and flex during transport. The battens can be removed and the walls then taped and textured once the home has been set up and has settled for a couple of weeks. Most dealers will provide for this option via inde-

Fig. 4.10.
Tongue-in-groove OSB flooring. (Photo courtesy Palm Harbor Homes.)

pendent contractors if you wish to pay for them to provide taping and texturing. Walls in wet areas (kitchen, baths and utility room) should retain their vinyl wallpaper and battens as the vinyl repels moisture, which is prevalent in these particular rooms. A few dealers market their homes with taping and texturing as a standard feature. While these walls have been taped and textured—definitely more elegant.

Fig. 4.11. Batten walls, typical for most cheaper homes.

Fig. 4.12. Taped and textured walls, giving a more residential look.

Ceilings

Ceilings have either fake texturing or are hand-textured. The fake texturing is much less expensive than hand texturing. Hand texturing adds a much more elegant appearance. The wall panels themselves are always made of fire-retardant gypsum board ("sheetrock").

Fig. 4.13. Roofing truss section being lowered onto the structure. (Photo courtesy Palm Harbor Homes.)

Fig. 4.14. Blowing insulation into a ceiling. (Photo courtesy Palm Harbor Homes.)

The insulation on top of your ceilings is normally blown in and is either a cellulose product or a product called "Rockwool" The latter is exactly what it's name portends: Steel and rocks are woven into a wool-like consistency creating a superior product that stays in place over time and won't settle into clumps. Rockwool is completely fire proof and is the best product of its type. The cellulose product, on the other hand, is a fire hazard, as it can ignite with enough heat. (Don't buy in to remarks or phony demonstrations that suggest otherwise).

Roofs

Roof construction on manufactured homes comes in three basic types: 2 in. x 2 in. birdcage either 16 in. OC (by far the most common) or 24 in. OC, 2 in. x 4 in. standard trusses (also either 16 in. OC or 24 in. OC) and steeper pitched hinged roofs which also utilize 2 in. x 4 in. trusses. Hinged roofs cost considerably more but give the home the look of a far more expensive site-built home. They can also provide attic space.

All roofs are decked with either plywood or (most likely) OSB. Particle-board is never used because of its obvious difficulties with wetness. Standard housing coverings are used for the roofing. Pe-

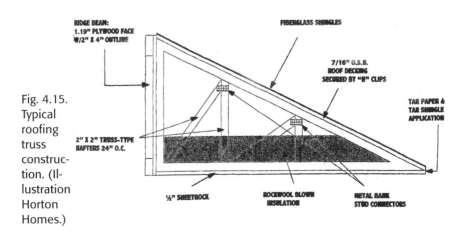

Fig. 4.15. Typical roofing truss construction. (Illustration Horton Homes.)

troleum based or fiberglass roof shingles are standard on the majority of manufactured homes, with petroleum based shingles being the most common. If choosing these shingles, be sure to obtain all warranty information. The weight and quality of these products can vary greatly.

Steel roofs (not to be confused with aluminum roofs, which are called metal roofs) are durable and extremely long-lived. These roofs are widely used in rural areas and are available in numerous colors. Not all manufacturers offer these coverings but, if you desire a steel roof, order your home with bare roof decking and have an independent contractor install it for you.

The roof's overhang will vary from one brand of house to the next and, in truth, doesn't matter as long as it sticks out at least 4 inches. Less overhang than that can allow moisture to accumulate in the upper walls and roofing base edges, which can cause serious problems in the future. Top-of-the-line homes have eaves that extend as far out as 12 inches, and those are aesthetically much more pleasing.

Fig. 4.16. Installing roof sheathing and tiles. (Photo courtesy of Palm Harbor Homes.)

Siding

A surprising number of manufacturers construct their homes without structural exterior wall sheathing, offering it only as an option. Just like roof decking, sheathing is almost always either plywood or OSB. It is best to pass up the purchase of a home with only foam-type sheathing since the structure is significantly weaker and has inadequate weatherproofing. A projectile, like a rock thrown by a nearby lawn mower, can literally pass through vinyl siding, insulation and sheetrock and strike something or someone inside the house. It would have a really hard time penetrating a sheet of plywood or OSB. Your normal siding choices include aluminum (generally single-wides only), Masonite, vinyl, Hardipanel (or very similar Maxipanel), Smart Panel (OSB) and log-like or plank cedar siding.

Split log siding is wonderful looking, particularly in rural settings.

With a lifetime warranty and never requiring painting, vinyl siding is a very popular choice.

Basic single-wides have metal (aluminum) siding and roofs. This covering is remarkably durable, but is not accepted by all manufactured home parks. Do not overlook this fact as you could

Fig. 4.17.
Home with
split log siding.

45

end up stuck with a house with no place to put it. If moving to the country, though, the low maintenance aspect of metal/metal can make it a very sound choice.

Masonite is the most widely used wood product siding utilized in the entire housing industry. It is similar to particle-board but is thinner and is coated with a water resistant barrier. Its advantages are its low cost, availability and general ease of maintenance. If not properly maintained, though, it can rot quickly, permitting damage to the inner structure. This siding should be inspected for rotting and loose caulking every 6 months, just to be on the safe side. Warranties are based upon manufacturing de-

Left: Fig. 4.18. Home with vinyl sided MH wall.

Below: Fig. 4.19. An old single-wide with corrugated metal siding and metal roof.

fects, primarily, and sectional replacement is often necessary within the life of the house.

Vinyl siding is quickly becoming the favorite choice of new home buyers. It's easily installed, is very attractive, never needs

Fig. 4.20. Bottom of the line kitchen sink plumbing without shutoff valves.

Fig. 4.21. With plastic shutoff valves, this arrangement is at least acceptable.

Fig. 4.22. High-quality, red colored hot water lines and brass shutoff valves. This will work best.

painting and has a lifetime warranty.

Smart panel is simply paint coated, sculpted OSB. Each panel actually functions as both sheathing and siding, making it remarkably efficient. It has only recently been introduced to the market, so you may have to ask your dealer about its availability.

Hardipanel (or Maxipanel) is another recent entry to the siding option list, but is already widely available. Consisting of cement mixed with glass fibers, this heavy material (which comes in sheets) cannot catch on fire, is impervious to bugs and caustic chemicals and is virtually bullet-proof. It makes the structure much heavier and will lower your insurance premiums because it's considered masonry.

Cedar siding is very attractive, particularly in rural settings. You can even find "log-like" versions. Cedar siding costs more than conventional sidings and must be chemically treated annually to prevent discoloration and decay. Treatment for a 2,000 square foot home takes under an hour and is well worth the effort and the low cost of maintenance.

Plumbing

Basic plumbing is pretty much the same throughout the industry, normally utilizing CPVC piping or Quest Pak (for flex lines), which has the highest rating. These are relatively flexible and re-

Fig. 4.23. All toilets *should* have shutoff valves, as shown here, too.

sist deterioration with the passing of time. However, there is an enormous difference in the sturdiness of the plumbing systems overall, depending upon the couplings, flex lines and, most importantly, the placement of shut-off valves. The best systems have brass couplings and reinforced flexible hoses running to all spigots, each with a brass shutoff valve. Lower quality valves are plastic. The shopper should inspect underneath all sinks. While looking under there, check the flooring at the base. These are the most likely areas for water damage, so particle-board, although it's frequently used here, is a poor choice anywhere near wet areas. OSB is the logical choice. It's also extremely important to have a main shutoff valve in an accessible location, most logically in the utility area. This can possibly prevent a disaster. If not quickly stopped, even a tiny leak can severely damage your home,

Fig. 4.24 Outside spigots are a useful option.

Fig. 4.25. Main water shutoff valves (the handle on the left) are featured in better homes.

potentially costing you thousands of dollars.

AC/Heating Registers

Of the three types of air conditioning/heating registers, the floor-mounted varieties are the most common in manufactured homes. Floor registers, although sometimes in the way of some furniture placements, are the most reliable and are the easiest to service. They also cost less to install.

Perimeter registers, which are placed by the floor moldings, are the most efficient at heating and cooling a building. They are much more convenient than floor registers, but cost more to install.

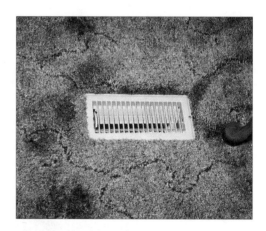

Fig. 4.26. Floor register.

Fig. 4.27. Ceiling register.

Although just a tiny bit less efficient, ceiling registers are completely out of the way and are preferred by many home buyers.

Each of the three register types is adequately efficient and any one of these choices is fine, as all three are virtually maintenance-free.

Electrical Wiring

While inspecting the utility room, take a look into the electric service box to determine the load capacity. If the stove, furnace and water heater use gas, a 100 amp service is more than adequate. If the house is all-electric, a 200 amp service is preferable for both safety and convenience. If you're planning to operate any high amperage shop equipment, then 200 amp service is a necessity.

HUD requires copper wiring throughout the house. The thickness of the wires is expressed in "gauge" number, with lower numbers corresponding to thicker wires:12-2 gauge wiring will be thicker, and safer, than 14-2 gauge. 10-2 gauge would be the safest. (The second number stands for the number of leads in the cable.)

Cabinets

Make sure that the upper kitchen cabinets are a full 12 inches deep, not only 10½ inches. Dinner plates are traditionally 11½

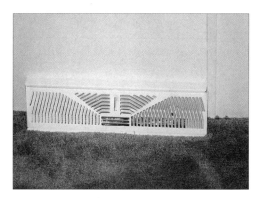

Fig. 4.28. Perimeter register.

inches in diameter, so they won't fit into those smaller, cheaper cabinets. This little matter can make a huge difference in terms of practical use.

Windows

Single pane windows come standard with most homes. They are prone to sweat and certainly don't insulate as well as storm windows or vinyl clad dual panes (generally called thermopanes), but they still easily fit HUD's requirements and perform reasonably well at keeping out the elements.

Dual-pane windows are attractive, efficient and wonderfully serviceable. They are also rather expensive. Dual pane windows are built of high impact plastic frames with two separate panes of glass a mere fraction of an inch apart with an invisible, insulating gas between them. These are excellent insulators for outside noises, as well as for temperature variants.

Fig. 4.29. Typical 200 Amp electrical service box.

Storm windows are not as attractive but are an extremely economical option. They insulate very well, don't tend to "sweat" and are simple to maintain and replace.

Carpets

Carpets come in many colors and designs. Solid weave carpets are more plush and luxurious, while sculptured carpets wear and hide stains better. A good carpet should have a weight rating of at least 16 ounces. Carpets that are lighter than these are pretty flimsy and don't last very long with normal, day-to-day traffic.

Above: Fig. 4.30. Trellis skirting.
Below: Fig. 4.31. Concrete block perimeter-foundation.

Carpet pads come in two basic forms: Foam and rebond. Foam is relatively short lived and turns into powder after only a few short years of moderately high traffic. Rebond, on the other hand, doesn't wear out at all and normally carries a warranty covering the life of the carpet. If you are offered a new version of foam padding that is supposed to be more durable, only accept it if it carries a warranty for the life of the carpet.

Skirting

Skirting is the covering for the structure's lower outside perimeter. All dealers offer it as an option, and I recommend you get it installed. It is designed to keep out critters and weather, but it must also "breathe," allowing moisture to escape, while also allowing access to the underside of the house for servicing.

You may prefer to utilize a type of skirting not offered by the dealer, such as stone masonry, stucco or trellis. Also, many zoning regulations now require manufactured homes to be placed upon permanent stone or masonry bases. The appearance of these homes is greatly enhanced, making them far more appealing to your neighbors. Conventional vinyl skirting, like the kind offered by most dealers, allows a great deal of air to circulate underneath

Fig. 4.32. Brick perimeter-foundation.

the structure, which is most effective at keeping the sub-flooring consistently dry. But, in the instance of a structural fire, this skirting allows for such a large volume of air circulation that the combustion process is greatly accelerated, negating a lot of the fire retardant qualities of the home. Therefore, it is my personal recommendation that a more solid and fire resistant material be used for skirting, implemented with reasonably spaced air vents. Be sure to hire a competent contractor to do this or consult your manufactured home dealer.

Decks, Porches, Etc.

Although most manufacturers offer decks and porches, on select models, as options from the factory, consider having these added on after setup by a contractor of your own choosing.

Most of the time you will spend far less, you won't be sacrificing floor space you're already paying for, and you can have it built exactly the way you'd like it to be.

Don't allow yourself to pass up on one of these "porch" models, though, if it truly satisfies your criteria. Also, make sure to insist

Fig. 4.33. Vinyl skirting.

that your dealer furnishes you with temporary steps. They shouldn't charge you for them.

Many discriminating manufactured home buyers opt to provide their own wall and floor coverings. This allows them to use any materials available without being limited to the factory's choices. They simply order the house "blue nailed," which means their home arrives with bare sheetrock walls and bare floor decking and, if desired, even bare roof decking and siding. There will only be a slight reduction in cost, but the sky's the limit on your choices.

Fig. 4.34. Factory-installed porch on a double-wide (shown before the gable siding is installed).

Fig. 4.35. A porch installed by an independent contractor.

Options For Your Home

The following is a list of common options that you may consider specifying with your home. Keep in mind that, even if there is extra cost involved, it will be cheaper to obtain the home with the options you will want rather than replacing or modifying these items after the fact (which in some cases will actually be impossible). Add to that the advantage of being able to finance the extra cost with a low-interest mortgage rather than by much more expensive short-term financing means.

- Custom cabinets
- Taped and textured interior walls
- Walk-in closets
- 2 in. x 6 in. exterior wall studs

Fig. 4.36. Exploded view of a well-built triple-wide. (Illustration courtesy Palm Harbor Homes.)

- Recessed tubs & whirlpools

- 2 in. x 4 in. interior wall studs, 16 in. OC

- Porcelain (vs. plastic) bathroom sinks

- Removable hitch

- Wood-burning or gas fireplaces

- Roof dormers

- Exterior siding upgrades

- Varying roof pitches

- Roof covering upgrades

- Attics (hinged roofs only)

- Hardwood flooring

- Additional exterior lighting

- Ceramic tile floors

- Additional exterior spigots

- Carpet and carpet pad upgrades

- Stone or masonry skirting

- Exterior door upgrades

- Additional porches and decks

- Additional exterior outlets

- Slate or marble foyers

- Window upgrades

- Skylights

- Insulation upgrades

- Built-in desks, hutches and bookshelves

- "Blue nailing"

- Upgrade appliance packages

- Additional appliances

- Interior moldings

- Adjustable shelves in closets

- Adjustable shelves in cabinets

- Real wood doors and cabinets

- Ceramic bathroom fittings

- Telephone and computer jacks

- Ceiling fans

- Room lighting upgrades

- Intercom/stereo systems

5. Understanding Warranties

JUST like with all other retail products, the warranties that come with your manufactured home and the equipment installed in it are only as good as the reputation of the manufacturer and/or the dealer. All manufacturers are required to include a one-year warranty with their homes and some offer up to five years. Some others will offer additional coverage for an additional sum of money. Since not all manufacturing defects become apparent within the first year, it's definitely advisable to purchase the longer-term warranty. Even so, you need a clear understanding of what is covered and what is not:

- Warranties **do** cover:

  - Workmanship in the structure

  - Factory installed plumbing, heating and electrical systems

  - Factory installed appliances, which may also be covered by separate appliance manufacturer warranties

- Warranties **don't** cover:

  - Improper installation and maintenance

- Accidents

- Owner negligence

- Unauthorized repairs

- Normal wear and aging

On your *Apples To Apples* and *Setup* checklists, you will find spaces for the names and telephone numbers of both the dealer service representative and the factory service representative. Failure on the part of the dealer to provide you with this information will be a dead giveaway that service is not a priority with this particular dealership. If this is the case, do not buy a home from them, no matter how tempting their products or offers may appear to be. Insist upon visiting the service department of each dealership and you will quickly discover exactly how "service oriented" this particular organization really is.

No matter how well your home is constructed, its setup and servicing can be the most important factors in determining the longevity and overall functionality of your home. Numerous short-cuts may be taken and, since good servicing becomes quite costly, a rare few unscrupulous dealers prefer to neglect their customers here (they already have your money) and get by as cheaply as possible by hiring under-qualified setup crews, utilizing cheaper, inferior materials and ignoring customers who have legitimate service complaints. Saving a few dollars up front doesn't necessarily mean you'll end up saving money in the long run. Negligent service can ultimately ruin an otherwise sound structure. If a dealership has a history of poor service, then the Better Business Bureau will most likely have some complaints on record. The majority of dealers provide credible service but, for your own sake, don't neglect to check them all out. Immediately eliminate any one of them that has more than a couple of complaints. Do not be swayed by tempting ads or fancy displays put out by that type of dealership. Don't take a chance by believing they've somehow miraculously "changed!"

6.

Selecting a Floor Plan

IT'S a good idea to have a basic perception as to what general layout, or floor plan, for your new home would fit your likes and needs. Look at these basic examples so you can give your sales rep an idea as to what you would like to consider. This will also acclimate you for examining each dealership's floor plans. It is recommended that you determine the number of bedrooms desired, as well as how you would like your common living areas, kitchen, bathroom, and utility areas to be situated.

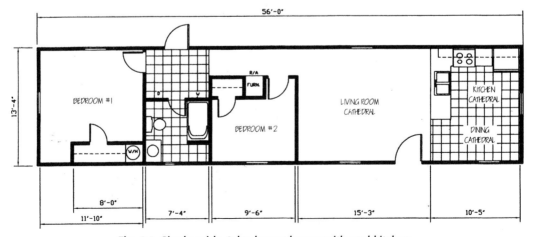

Fig. 6.1. Single-wide 2-bedroom home with end kitchen.

If you wish to order your home from the factory, I would recommend choosing the proper basic floor plan, taking it home and penciling in options you would like in your new manufactured home. You may look over the section in this book entitled "Common Options." You should also acquire your dealer's list of their options, including their costs. Factories cannot necessarily facilitate additional, unlisted option wishes as readily as many site-built contractors because, in order to keep prices down on a per unit basis, manufactured homes must apply the options listed by the dealers only. Slowing down production raises costs, so their reasoning is purely logical.

Most home designs can be mirrored, or flipped. Fireplaces, optional doors, both interior and exterior, can be placed in numerous places, as well as ceiling fans, chandeliers, computer, cable-tv and telephone outlets. Plumbing, electrical wiring and heat/AC vents aren't moveable. Sometimes windows and doors can be added, and sometimes they cannot. Porches may replace some rooms, and vice-versa. Be keenly aware of all up-grade packages and all other available options. If you don't ask, you may never know.

Single-Wide Floor Plans

Single-wides offer the ultimate in economy, and if your budget and need for space are modest, you should consider one of these. Most

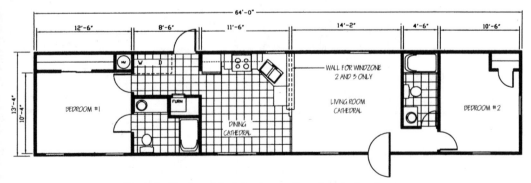

Fig. 6.2. Single-wide 2-bedroom "mother-in-law" setup.

of the original trailer coaches had the kitchen/dining area located in front of the structure, just behind the hitch. This allowed for all kitchen plumbing, along with propane tanks, to be in one serviceable location. Located behind this area is a small living section and a bathroom next in line. When the need for more space became necessary for more purchasers of these objects, an additional bedroom was added onto the rear. Trailer parks all over our nation have countless variations of this design. With an excellent outdoor view from the kitchen and from the rear bedroom, this design can still be found in the brochures and on the lots of numerous manufacturers. Although no longer a huge seller, 2 bedroom single-wides with front kitchens should remain on the market for many years to come. These are absolutely ideal for hunters and sportsmen of all types and can be found in numerous remote locations. With liquid propane tanks and an electricity generator, this is a superior home away from home or great for small parks.

Family living and the desire for parental privacy most likely played a hand in the original "mother-in-law" setup, which separates the bedrooms from one another by placing them on either end of the home (see Fig. 6.2). This is a typical layout offered by most manufacturers of 2-bedroom single-wides. This simple configuration comes in numerous lengths. These economical homes are found in manufactured housing communities around the country.

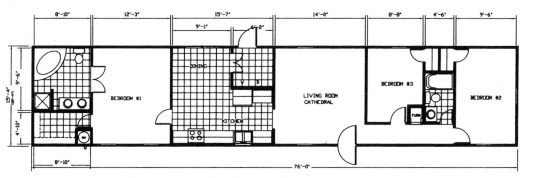

Fig. 6.3. Typical 3-bedroom, 2-bathroom single-wide.

On a three-bedroom, 2-bath single-wide, the master bedroom and master bath are on the left, with the utility room, kitchen, and living room in the center, and the entry door opening into the living room, while the two minor bed rooms and bathroom are on the right, as shown in Fig. 6.3. The kitchen layout has numerous variations, as do the master bath and utility room, but the fundamental layout is seldom different. The master bath in all higher-end models is spacious and useful. You can find this type of home in lengths varying from 56 feet up to 80 feet. If you don't require an extremely large amount of floor-space, you just may want to consider checking out some of these larger single-wide homes. Be sure to look at more than just a couple.

Double-Wide Floor Plans

Being constructed in several sections, there is increased set-up and foundation cost involved in a double-wide. However, it's a great way to get a spacious home with a more residential look.

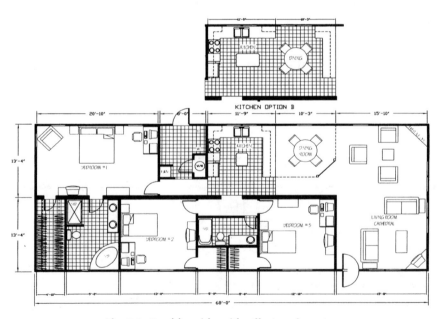

Fig. 6.4. Double-wide with offset main entry.

With the layout shown in Fig. 6.4, the great room (that's a modern real-estate term for what used to be called the living room) is located on one end of the home, while the formal entry is in the front of the structure, off-set to the right. Of course, all floor plans can be mirrored, or flipped, which, in this case, would place the great room on the left. Whenever the living area covers an entire end of

Fig. 6.5. Double-wide with entry hallway and numerous notable options.

Fig.

6.6.

Fig. 6.6. Double-wide with typical 3-bedroom, 2-bathroom family setup.

the home, all bedrooms are adjacent, "family style." It is simple and aesthetically pleasing to add on a deck or a porch at the right side and on the right front of the house. Being on the gable portion

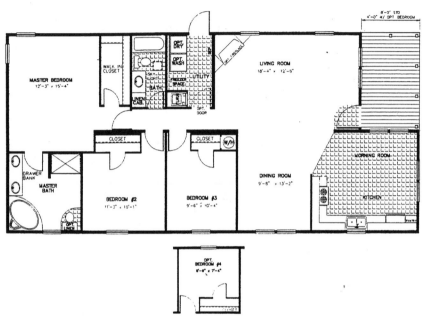

Fig. 6.7. Double-wide with great room and main entryway on one end.

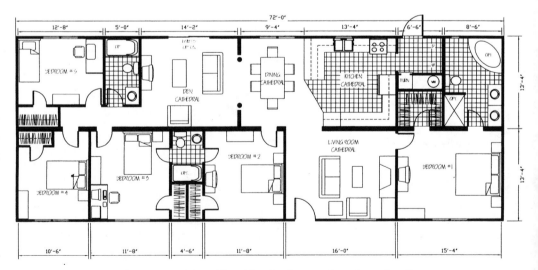

Fig. 6.8. Double-wide with 5 bedrooms for a large family.

of the structure, very large windows could be mounted in the living area exterior wall. This is especially attractive if the house overlooks a pleasing vista.

Numerous options allow the manufactured home buyers to order their homes with a plethora of variations. The layouts shown in Figs. 6.6 through 6.8 show double-wides that can be modified from the original 3 bedroom, 2 bath configuration to have up to 4 or 5 bedrooms, 3 or 4 bedrooms with a retreat or office, and/or a secure entry hallway. Many things can be done within the confines of a basic rectangular box.

Parents with young children may prefer to sleep close enough to their kids to keep tabs on them. The floor plan shown in Fig. 6.6 utilizes the "family setup," which places all three bedrooms adjacent to one another on one end of the house. Notice the optional patio door, which allows for side access into the den. Patio doors — either sliding glass or French doors — are almost always offered as options and may be placed in practically any room leading outside. Fireplaces are another option and can be placed in numerous locations, depending upon your preference.

Be it for curbside appeal, placement for a view or simply one's preference, most all manufacturers offer homes with the formal entry on one end of the home, as opposed to being placed at the

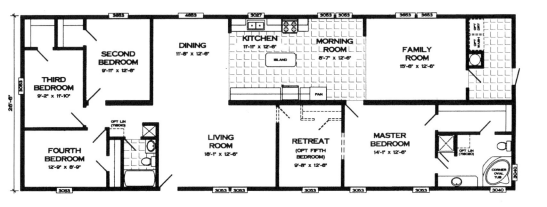

Fig. 6.9. Double-wide with multiple options: 4, 5, or even 6-bedroom potential.

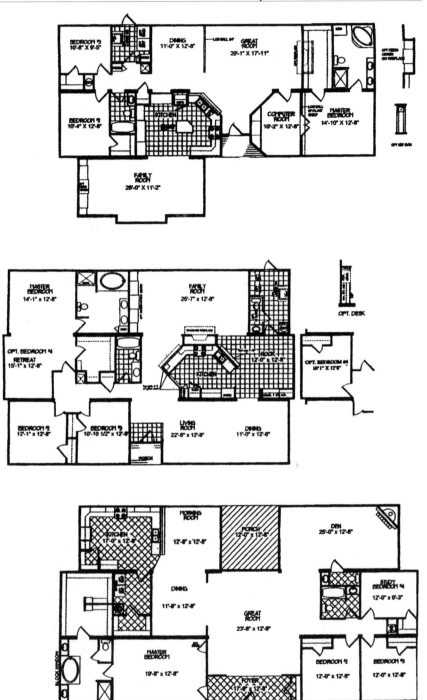

Figs. 6.10, 6.11, and 6.12. Three triple-wide floor plans.

front of the long side of the structure. There can definitely be advantages to this configuration, but if you order your home with this basic design, you can normally forget about having the "mother-in-law" setup, which places the master bedroom on the opposite side of the house from the other bedrooms. There are

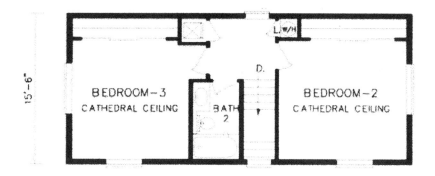

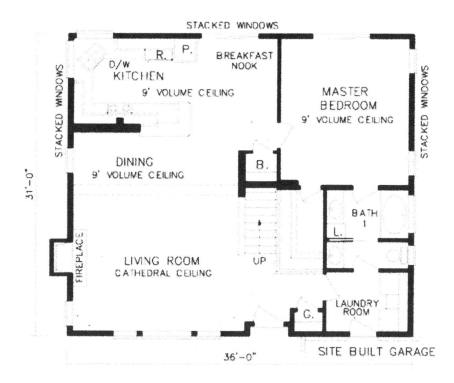

Fig. 6.13. Two-story triple-wide.

countless situations where this design is a preferable choice.

In layouts like those of Fig. 6.5, 6.6, 6.8, and 6.9, Mom and Dad can enjoy some privacy from the kids in their master bedroom, which is located on the opposite end of the house from the other bedrooms. In Fig. 6.8 the kids share a den and two bathrooms. Notice the identical bedrooms sharing a common bathroom between them. These are called "Hansel and Gretel rooms" and are ideal for twins or siblings of near equal ages. The living room, which is accessed through the main entry, is farther away from the den and the children's rooms, which helps keep it tidy. A sliding glass door in the den leads to the back yard.

In the layout per Fig. 6.9, there's lots of space, with three kids' rooms and a master bedroom with a retreat, or if desired, a fourth

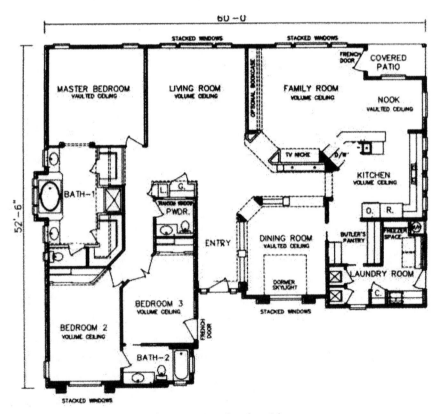

Fig. 6.14. Quadruple-wide.

bedroom in place of the retreat for a small infant. Also, the family room can function as a large bedroom. Many families can't afford a site-built home with this much space, but a manufactured home fulfills their needs for living space and privacy. Notice the kitchen has an island, which facilitates the preparation of large meals. There is a morning room by the family room (or 6th bedroom), as well as a separate dining room. This is a relatively common floor plan. Notice, also, that there is ample space for a freezer in the utility room. It's usually possible to add another bath or half bath in the utility room, if desired.

Triple-Wide, Quadruple-Wide, and 2-Story Floor Plans

Triple-wides are almost always comprised of two full-length sections and a smaller, additional section. The design shown in Fig. 6.12 places the kitchen section in the back portion of the home. It could also be a bedroom, a den, or an auxiliary room, which can be ordered for the front, rear or on either end. With a huge great room appreciated upon entering the home, the addition of a visible extended kitchen section provides a truly appreciable amount of spaciousness. Triple-wides are available nationwide.

Yes, two-story manufactured homes are a reality. Since the turn of the 21st century, the sky has become the limit for multi-sectional homes. With these two-story structures, the second floor section is lifted up by a crane and securely attached to the top of the first level. It would be virtually impossible to distinguish these fantastic homes from a much more expensive site-built home. Contractor added attachments, such as garages, carports, etc., are almost always included in the sale of the home. You hardly have to worry about zoning restrictions with homes like these.

Covering nearly 3,000 square feet, the quadruple-wide home shown in Fig. 6.12 would impress anybody. Trailer home? Please. Genuine luxury at an economic rate is the reward for anyone ordering one of these beauties. There's lots of room for porches and decks, added onto the frames at the factory. Ditto for bedroom configurations.

7. Financing Your Home

There are two ways of paying for your manufactured home: Either you can pay for it all at once ("cash"), or you pay a percentage up front and then pay off the balance in increments ("financing"). When you finance your home you will also pay interest, which can cost you a lot more than the original purchase price of the house. When you pay cash for a $65,000.00 home, the total amount you will pay is $65,000.00. When you finance that same home through a 20-year loan with 10% down at a modest annual interest rate of 7¼%, the total amount you will pay is $110,877,26. If there are certain derogatory statements on your credit report, and if you're applying to a conventional, name-brand lender, your interest rate could be as high as 15%, (this is a very rough figure). In this case you will end up paying $184,877.26 for that same $65,000.00 house.

First and foremost, if you are planning to finance your home, you should apply at a reputable lender *before* looking for the home. Being pre-approved by a respected lender will prevent the possible chance of being ripped off of additional funds in the form of inordinate points and kick-backs to maverick lenders and dealers. If your credit is in good shape, do this first!

I realize, though, that this advice will seldom be heeded, and in consequence financing will occur through a lender of the dealership's choosing. Some dealerships utilize some very good lenders, but even in the best-case scenario, you lose control of the financing process.

If you hold title to a used manufactured home, which appraises for around $8,000.00 or more, you can save a few thousand dollars while using that home as a trade-in. Coming up with a few thousand dollars for a down payment shouldn't be necessary. If that home is worth less than around $8,000.00 it can still be used as a trade-in, with no down payment needed. Take note, though, that this amount will most likely not come off the purchase price. If you still owe on your trade-in, its payoff can be added into the financing, but unless you owe very little, this home should be sold separately. Any competent dealer will be most eager to help you do this since they will profit from selling one of their homes to you, once yours is sold. They will also most likely get a higher price for your home than you could. Everyone comes out ahead—so why not?

If you don't have a few thousand dollars available and you don't have a used home for trade, or if you don't hold title to any land, most dealers will take in cars, trucks, boats, motorcycles, RVs or other items of value. It's an excellent idea to compile a list of all items you can possible use to make a down payment. A few dealerships will even let a buyer apply "sweat equity," which is providing labor or some other service for which the dealership will pay them in lieu of part or all of their down payment.

"Zero Down Payment" is a seriously misleading come-on because zero down payment options are available only to buyers who either own some land outright and will agree to offer their deed as collateral for their home financing ("land-in-lieu"), or they have more than substantial income and impeccable credit. Land-in-lieu is scary, since foreclosure can leave one both homeless *and* landless. Under the proper circumstances, though, this procedure can be a worthwhile risk. A buyer who has excellent credit and substantial income *should* pay as large a down payment as possible because the higher the down payment, the lower the interest rate and payments.

How's Your Credit?

Most Americans have average to below average credit. If you find yourself in this majority, take heart. Don't let sub-par credit deter you from applying for a loan on a manufactured home. But... keep in mind that each and every time you contact a credit bureau to inquire about your credit, your credit "score" (Beacon or Empirica) is lowered by a few points, making a loan less certain. More than 6 inquiries over a 12 month period will turn away many lenders, so limit your inquiries to the final home of your choosing.

Unless you're paying cash for your home, do not yield to the temptation of setting a foot onto a single sales lot until you have acquired your own copy of your credit report from all three bureaus. You can begin the process of acquiring all three of these reports at the same time by dialing the following toll-free number: 1-888-567-8688. You will be required to include a photocopy of your driver's license and, most likely, a utility bill to prove you're whom you claim to be. By law, a dealer cannot give you a copy of the report they obtained on you. I can't emphasize this enough: Get your own credit reports!

Occasionally, incorrect information is mistakenly put on your report. It can happen to anyone. If you find an erroneous report, contact that bureau immediately. It will take at least 30 days for them to delete it from your records, so take care of this matter well before ever physically shopping for your manufactured home.

Some dealerships will not allow you to even look at one of their homes unless they have run your credit. Since most "lookers" aren't actually "buyers," It's understandable that the sales person can't be expected to make a living as a tour guide for unqualified lookers who are merely curiosity seekers. Explain to that sales person that you're neither a "tire-kicker" nor a "get-me-bought," that you have your own credit report from each bureau and you will allow her/him to look them over. If they still insist on running their own credit check, then tell them you will buy your home from a dealer who does accept your credit report.

Once you have decided upon your new home (this is if you're not paying cash, of course) you must allow them to run your credit for themselves, as this is always required by the lenders. Your credit score will be higher and your interest rate (and payments) may even be slightly lower if you'll just follow these common-sense guidelines.

If you have any unpaid government loans (including student loans), delinquent child support payments, unpaid utilities or ugly banking references (all lenders are banks and will stick together) don't expect to have your loan approved until these problems are cleared up. Bankruptcies, repossessions, liens or judgments may eliminate conventional lenders, but there are countless high APR/high-points lenders who may be more than willing to take a chance on you—providing your income can cover your installments and you can provide a healthy down payment. Some dealerships carry their own paper, meaning they operate as their own banks and they might possibly finance your home for you. Just be sure to carefully read your contracts and keep copies of everything you and they have agreed upon and signed. This is known as "owner financing" and is, for many buyers, the only chance for obtaining financing.

All lenders expect the borrower to have enough money after all other bills have been paid to be able to afford their mortgage payment. The term for this is "budgeting." There are numerous formulas which they can use, but the simplest way to determine if you budget is to check whether your monthly home loan payment does not exceed 21% of your gross income minus all other loan payments. If your payment is $350.00 per month and you only gross $275.00 per week, then you probably don't budget, according to whatever formula they use and, with those numbers, your financing won't be approved. You will have to change your strategy or shop for a less expensive home.

Home price$50,000	$75,000	$100,000	$150,000
Rate		Necessary income	
6%	$16,754	$25,131	$33,508	$50,261
6.5%	$17,451	$26,176	$34,901	$52,352
7%	$18,163	$27,244	$36,325	$54,488
7.5%	$18,889	$28,334	$37,779	$56,668
8%	$19,630	$29,445	$39,260	$58,889
8.5%	$20,383	$30,574	$40,766	$62,149
9%	$21,148	$31,722	$42,296	$63,444
9.5%	$21,925	$32,887	$43,849	$65,774
10%	$22,711	$34,067	$45,423	$68,134
10.5%	$23,508	$35,262	$47,016	$70,523
11%	$24,313	$36,470	$48,626	$72,940
11.5%	$25,127	$37,690	$50,254	$75,380

How Much Do You Need to Earn?

Here is a common chart used by a large number of dealerships to aid in determining if the buyer can afford a particular manufactured home, financing it with a 30-year loan with 20% down, as well as the inclusion of normal taxes, delivery, setup, additional contractor costs and insurance payments:

Banks all use simple, logical formulas to determine an applicant's eligibility for loan approval. Since you had to live someplace before, they want to know how well you took care of your previous mortgage or rent, as well as that particular property. Since they're all banks, they want to know how you've treated *other* banks. Since you must earn an income in order to pay your bills, they need to know how steady and secure you are at earning this income. Since most people encounter problems which can affect their credit ratings, they will accept reasonable (and provable) explanations, most particularly when it concerns medical bills.

There are numerous government-funded lenders who are willing to lend monies to persons with poor credit as long as certain criteria are met. The Federal Housing Authority (FHA) is the most prominent of these lenders. In most, if not all cases, they will handle land/home applications only. If you already have land on which to place your home, or if you'll be renting a space, this would be a chattel loan and might not qualify you for government funding. Many single-wides have been purchased via chattel loans with the purchasers placing these in mobile home parks. If repossession has been requested by the lender, it is very easy for one of the repo crews to just pull up to the unit and remove it. Since it would also be just as easy for the purchaser to have this unit removed and placed where it couldn't be found, it is becoming more and more difficult to acquire a chattel loan. In fact, by 2005 all chattel loans will most likely be completely extinct. However, if you wish to finance a portion of land along with your manufactured home, then you should have an excellent chance of obtaining approval. New lending plans are coming out all the time, so if you're not seeking a land/home situation, have your dealer search for suitable funding. Government loans generally take much longer to process than conventional loans, but they're easier to acquire and their interest rates are extremely competitive. You must budget and begin the process of repaying all creditors who have reported you to be in arrears.

Probably the last resort for financing your home is for a friend or relative who has suitable credit to either provide a co-signature for the loan or to apply with you as a "buy-for." With a co-signature this person assumes responsibility for the entire term of your loan. A "buy-for" is much better for this person because all responsibility for this loan reverts back to you after 12 to 24 months, provided you've made your payments in a timely manner. The better their credit, the less interest you'll have to pay. This will also aid in repairing and building your credit.

There are numerous plans offered by lenders, so be sure to study your options before deciding which one is best for you.

Many dealers use come-ons like "No Turndowns," "All Applications Accepted," "No Refusals" and various other plays on words. Of course they won't refuse or turn down your application. That doesn't mean that a lender will approve your loan. Remember: Around 40%

down will get practically *any* applicant a loan for their home, so basically everyone is "approved."

Absolutely *do not* fill out a credit application until you have made your final decision on the exact home you wish to buy.

When you have decided to submit a credit application, be prepared by having the following items on hand:

- Current driver's license, state ID card or passport

- Social Security card

- Current utility bills

- Checking and savings account information

- Last 2 years W-2's (annual earnings statements)

- Previous 2 years income tax returns

- Last 2 paycheck stubs

- Credit card numbers, limits, payment amounts and balances

- Names, addresses, phone numbers, initial loan amounts and balances of all other creditors

- Names, addresses and phone numbers of two friends or relatives who don't live with you

- 5 years employment history including company names, addresses, phone numbers, supervisor, hire and leaving dates and starting and ending pay

- 5 years residence history including landlord or lender, rent or mortgage payments and all pertinent contact names, addresses and phone numbers

- Any additional financial information including social security, SSI, retirement funds, stocks, bonds or other annuities, child support payments, bankruptcy discharge documents, divorce judgment documents or anything else affecting your financial situation

• A complete list of literally everything of value that you own.

Don't be lazy and trust that things will just "work out." Failure to dig up and provide this information can easily cause your loan approval to be delayed for days, weeks or even months—or quite possibly leave the lenders with no choice but to decline your loan.

How Much Will You Actually Pay?

On the following pages are charts providing the payment amounts for your mortgage payments. The amount financed is the selling price of the house, along with all other costs you will incur, minus your down payment. The table only goes up to $100,000, but it can easily be used to figure your payment on greater amounts. To give two simple examples, multiply the figure for $100,000 by two to get the payment for a $200,000 loan, or add the figures for $100,000 and $25,000 to get the payments for a $125,000 loan.

6% Annual Percentage Rate

Loan term (years)	10	15	20	25	30
Amount Financed			Monthly Payment ($)		
$25,000	277.56	210.97	179.11	161.08	149.90
$30,000	333.07	253.16	214.93	193.30	179.87
$35,000	388.58	295.36	250.75	225.51	209.86
$40,000	444.09	337.55	286.58	257.73	239.83
$45,000	499.00	379.74	322.40	289.94	269.80
$50,000	555.11	421.93	358.22	322.16	299.78
$60,000	666.13	506.32	429.86	386.59	359.74
$70,000	777.15	590.70	501.51	451.02	419.69
$80,000	888.17	675.09	573.15	515.45	479.65
$90,000	999.19	759.48	644.79	579.88	539.60
$100,000	1,110.21	843.86	716.14	644.31	599.56

7% Annual Percentage Rate

Loan term (years)	10	15	20	25	30
Amount Financed		**Monthly Payment ($)**			
$25,000	290.28	224.71	193.83	176.70	166.33
$30,000	348.33	269.65	232.59	212.04	199.60
$35,000	406.38	314.59	271.36	247.38	232.86
$40,000	464.44	359.54	310.12	282.72	266.13
$45,000	522.49	505.48	348.89	318.06	299.39
$50,000	580.55	449.42	387.65	353.39	332.66
$60,000	696.66	539.30	465.18	424.07	399.19
$70,000	812.76	629.18	542.71	494.75	465.72
$80,000	928.87	719.07	620.24	565.43	532.25
$90,000	1,044.98	808.95	696.77	636.11	598.78
$100,000	1,161.09	898.83	775.30	706.78	665.31

8% Annual Percentage Rate

Loan term (years)	10	15	20	25	30
Amount Financed		**Monthly Payment ($)**			
$25,000	303.32	238.91	209.11	192.95	183.44
$30,000	363.98	286.70	250.93	231.54	220.13
$35,000	424.65	334.48	292.75	270.14	256.82
$40,000	485.31	382.26	334.58	308.73	293.51
$45,000	545.97	505.48	348.89	318.06	299.39
$50,000	606.64	477.83	418.22	385.91	266.88
$60,000	727.97	573.39	501.86	463.09	440.26
$70,000	949.29	668.96	585.51	540.27	513.64
$80,000	970.62	764.52	669.15	617.45	587.01
$90,000	1,091.95	860.09	752.80	694.63	660.39
$100,000	1,238.28	898.83	775.30	706.78	665.31

9% Annual Percentage Rate

Loan term (years)	10	15	20	25	30
Amount Financed			Monthly Payment ($))		
$25,000	316.69	253.57	224.93	209.80	201.16
$30,000	389.03	304.28	268.92	251.76	241.39
$35,000	443.36	354.99	314.90	293.72	281.62
$40,000	506.70	405.71	359.89	335.68	321.85
$45,000	570.04	456.42	404.88	377.64	362.08
$50,000	633.38	507.13	449.86	419.60	402.31
$60,000	760.05	608.56	539.84	503.52	482.77
$70,000	886.73	709.99	629.81	587.44	563.24
$80,000	1,013.47	811.41	719.78	671.36	643.70
$90,000	1,140.08	912.84	803.75	755.28	724.16
$100,000	1,266.76	1,014.27	899.73	839.20	804.62

10% Annual Percentage Rate

Loan term (years)	10	15	20	25	30
Amount Financed			Monthly Payment ($)		
$25,000	330.38	268.55	241.26	227.18	219.39
$30,000	396.45	322.38	289.51	272.61	263.27
$35,000	462.53	376.11	337.76	318.05	307.15
$40,00	528.60	429.84	386.01	363.48	351.03
$45,000	594.68	473057	434.26	408.92	394.91
$50,000	660.75	537.30	482.51	454.35	438.79
$60,000	660.75	537.30	482.51	454.35	438.79
$70,000	925.06	752.22	675.52	636.09	614.30
$80,000	1,057.20	859.68	772.02	726.06	702.06
$90,000	1,189.36	967.14	868.52	817.83	789.81
$100,000	1,312.51	1,074.61	965.02	908.02	877.57

11% Annual Percentage Rate

Loan term (years)	10	15	20	25	30
Amount Financed			Monthly Payment ($)		
$25,000	344.38	284.15	258.05	245.03	238.08
$30,000	413.25	340.98	309.66	294.03	285.70
$35,000	482.13	397.81	361.27	343.04	333.31
$40,000	551.00	454.64	412.88	394.05	380.93
$45,000	619.88	511.47	464.48	441.05	428.55
$50,000	688.75	568.30	516.09	490.06	476.16
$60,000	826.50	681.96	619.31	588.07	571.39
$70,000	964.25	795.62	722.53	688.08	666.63
$80,000	1,102.00	909.28	825.75	784.09	761.86
$90,000	1,239.75	1,022.94	928.97	882.19	857.09
$100,000	1,377.50	1,136.60	1,032.19	980.11	852.32

12% Annual Percentage Rate

Loan term (years)	10	15	20	25	30
Amount Financed			Monthly Payment ($)		
$25,000	358.68	300.04	275.27	263.31	257.15
$30,000	430.41	360.05	330.33	315.97	308.58
$35,000	502.15	420.06	385.38	368.63	360.01
$40,000	573.88	480.07	440.43	421.29	411.45
$45,000	645.62	540.08	495.49	473.95	462.88
$50,000	717.35	600.08	550.54	526.61	514.31
$60,000	860.83	720.10	660.65	631.93	617.17
$70,000	1,004.30	840.12	770.76	737.26	720.03
$80,000	1,147.77	960.13	880.87	842.58	822.89
$90,000	1,291.24	1,080.15	990.98	947.90	925.75
$100,000	1,434.71	1,200.17	1,101.09	1,053.22	1,028.61

13% Annual Percentage Rate

Loan Term (years)	10	15	20	25	30
Amount Financed			Monthly Payment ($)		
$25,000	373.28	316.31	292.89	281.96	276.55
$30,000	447.93	379.57	351.47	338.35	331.86
$35,000	522.59	442.83	410.05	394.74	387.17
$40,000	597.24	506.10	468.63	451.13	442.48
$45,000	671.90	569.36	527021	507.63	497.79
$50,000	746.55	632.62	585.79	563.92	553.10
$60,000	895.86	759.15	702.95	676.70	663.72
$70,000	1,045.18	885.67	820.10	789.48	774.34
$80,000	1,194.49	1,012.19	937.26	902.27	884.96
$90,000	1,343.80	1,138.72	1,054.42	1,015.05	995.58
$100,000	1,493.11	1,265.24	1,171.58	1,127.84	1,106.20

It doesn't take a math genius to figure out that the lower the interest rate, the better value will be the home. A $50,000.00 mortgage at 6% APR to be paid in 30 years will require monthly payments of $299.78, resulting in a total amount of $107,920.80 paid for that home. This same mortgage amount and term at 13% APR will require monthly payments of $553.10, resulting in a total amount of $199,116.00 paid for that same home. That's a difference of $91,195.20. So it clearly makes sense to shop for the best rate possible.

Many lenders will allow you to lower your interest rate by selling you points. One point equals one per cent of the finance amount. This will raise your closing cost and ends up being added on to your finance amount so, obviously, I definitely don't recommend buying points to lower your interest rate unless it is absolutely the last resort for making your purchase feasible.

What Type of Loan Should You Apply For?

By far the most common mortgages acquired are long term, fixed rate loans (20 to 30 years). These allow for slightly lower payments, but may carry slightly higher interest rates. In most instances, I would recommend this type of loan.

Short term, fixed rate loans (15 years or less) are more cost effective if you can afford the payments. Interest rates should be a little lower and your equity will build up much faster. Excellent credit and a sizable down payment will save the largest amount of money for a buyer who intends to keep this home indefinitely.

Many lenders recommend Adjustable Rate Mortgage loans, or ARMs. Their rates vary with the economy and can potentially raise (or lower) your payments considerably. They may be a good deal when rates are high but not when they are low, because in the latter case your rate is likely to go up, and you may find yourself unable to pay.

If you apply for one of these mortgages, be sure there is a cap on the rate. ARMs are generally advantageous only for short-term investments, such as the purchase of properties that are bought to re-sell before the rates increase. This way, the borrower never realizes a raise in rates and thus profits from the entire transaction by saving on the early lower payments. In fairness, ARMs are sometimes the only way that some people can qualify for any loan at all, so prudent thinking is necessary in order to consider using this type of loan. Should you purchase a manufactured home via an ARM, or must you pass on your home altogether?

Graduated interest loans are normally the easiest to qualify for and are supposedly designed to require payment increases in chorus with normally figured average income increases. From my experience, these loans often lead to trouble unless the intent of the purchase is the same as that of most ARM borrowers, which is to turn over the property for a profit before interest rates are elevated.

My least favorite are balloon rate mortgages. For a specified time, payments are extremely reasonable. Basically, your payments cover all of the interest, and the final, or balloon payment, pays off the entire purchase amount. These, too, are fundamentally useful only for short-term borrowers who intend to sell before large amounts of money are required by the lender.

Do not put a foot onto a sales lot until you are *fully prepared* to buy a home. *Do your homework first*.

8. Where To Put Your Manufactured Home

L ET'S be certain to keep the horse in front of the cart: A home, whether manufactured or not, has to be placed somewhere, and it had better be somewhere you want to live. Far too many manufactured home buyers — like 9 out of 10 — don't seem to have considered the question as to where they are going to place their home, how much that property will cost them, or how it will be financed. One of the most asked questions I heard while assisting these folks was, "Do you have land?"

All dealerships have access to properties, developers, and real estate companies. Some even own land themselves, and in many cases they're only too eager to sell you a lot.

The problem is that most shoppers approach this situation blindly, by not having any idea about where they wish to live. By all means make it a point to locate your property first.

How? Take a walk through your yellow pages directory and contact numerous real estate agents. Explain what you're looking for and how much you think you can spend. Fill up your gas tank, visit real estate folks, and look, look, look.

Pinpoint your logistical needs and desires. How far from work are you prepared to live? If schools are an issue, their locations and quality must be known, as well as bus routes. Would you like to live in the country? Do you prefer to live in a subdivision or would you rather enjoy living more privately? Can you afford acreage or do you need minimal payments? What are the local zoning laws? (Your agent can find out for you) What utilities are available to that property?

Will you need a well and septic tank or will you be able to hook up to municipal water and a sewage system? What are the costs of providing those utilities? How well does each property drain? Does the property owner require cash or will she/he be willing to owner finance? Owner financing doesn't affect the amount of funds a bank will lend you for your home, but a conventional loan will lower the amount a lender will let you have to buy a manufactured home. Also, bad credit may force you to seek owner-financed lands exclusively.

You should have looked at enough properties to have at least two potential choices. Don't act on the purchase until you've found the right home. Remember: Manufactured home dealers will most likely only help you with properties that will benefit them to sell, and only if you buy a home from them. They might have the ideal spot for your home, but you're severely limiting your choices if you don't have a couple of properties already picked out.

Many buyers opt to place their homes in mobile home communities (no, they're not called "trailer parks" any more, but the idea is the same). In some you are required to purchase the plot for your home from the owners. In others, though, you can lease the land upon which you'll have your home placed. If you decide to do the latter (and it's better not to consider leasing your land, particularly if you purchase a double-wide), first make sure you can easily afford those lease payments. Bad things often happen when you don't own the land upon which you've placed your home. Nearly all of these "communities" have a long list of restrictions.

On the next page is a form that can be used to compare the essential data for the various lots you're considering for purchase:

Property Data Summary		
Selling Price $_____	**Financing:** Owner Financing @ _____ % for _____ months down payment: $	___ Cash or bank loan required
Lot size: _____ Acres _____ Square feet	Adjoining roads paved? _____	Does zoning permit manufactured homes? _____
Improvements		
Water: ____ Has well ____ Needs well Cost $_____	Electric: ____ Has pole ____ Needs pole Cost $_____	Waste Water: ____ Has septic tank ____ Needs septic tank Cost $_____
___ Has municipal water hookup ___ Needs municipal water hookup Cost $_____		___ Is hooked up to sewer system ___ Needs hookup to sewer system Cost $_____
Comments regarding schools: _____ _____	Comments regarding shopping: _____ _____	Comments regarding neighborhood: _____ _____

It's a great temptation to look at all those nice manufactured homes first and then hope to find a place to set it up, but don't do this. Knowing where to place your home should provide you with essential information that will aid you in determining which home to buy and how good a deal you're getting.

Foundation and Site Preparation

Moisture will damage or destroy any wooden structure and manufactured homes can be particularly vulnerable when placed in low-lying areas. For this reason, well before your home is delivered you will need to decide its exact placement. The ground underneath must either slope slightly or it must be "crowned" (like most highways) so that water has no possible chance of standing underneath the structure. Evaporating water permeates all wood and can eventually cause rotting and allow molds and mildews to flourish, damaging your home as well as being potentially harmful to the health of the occupants.

Many new manufactured home buyers assume that a solid concrete slab is the most desirable foundation base upon which to place their homes. Slabs are very heavy and strong and, because they are relatively expensive, most contractors will happily go along with the idea. In many metropolitan areas, slabs are (unfairly) required foundation bases for manufactured homes. Always be aware of all zoning regulations before choosing a foundation for your new home. If you would prefer to lay down a similarly effective but less costly foundation base, and zoning rules permit doing so, consider having a pad of gravel or road base

Don't grade the site so that water can collect in deep spots under the house

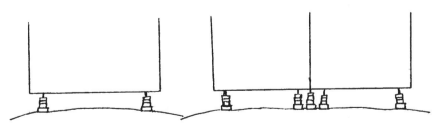

Grade the site so that it slopes down and away from the center of the house
Cover the ground underneath with 6 mil or thicker polyethylene sheeting.

Fig. 8.1 Sloping suggestions (note: 1 mil = 0.001 inch)

laid down. Then have concrete runners poured as pier supports, each one running the entire length of the structure or, if your contractor prefers, from front to back. There should be a row of runners for each set of piers, approximately 6 feet apart. The more numerous the piers, the sturdier the structure. Soil base and the weight of the structure will be determining factors for the dimensions of the runners. On top of the runners sit the piers. Most piers are comprised of standard concrete blocks sitting atop 2 in. x 1 6 in. x 16 in. concrete footings or ABS (plastic) pads. The least costly piers are steel jack stands. They're reasonably stable but definitely inferior to the other types of piers.

It is always best to utilize an FHA approved foundation. Not only will you be assured of the soundest possible support for your home but, if you ever desire to sell your home where it sits, your buyer will be able to acquire an FHA loan. Nationwide, 80% of all land/home loans for manufactured houses are secured through FHA, although in some states many dealerships have managed to

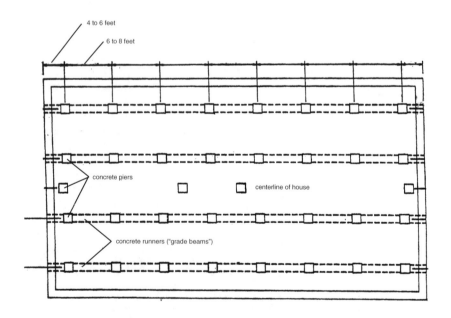

Fig. 8.2. Overview layout of piers and runners.

avoid this method of lending. Never, ever allow your home to be set up on top of bare ground! This cost saving move will almost certainly bring on the ruination of your home.

Rebar-reinforced concrete runners with concrete block piers run underneath the length of the home. Steel bands attached to I-beams on the upper ends and attached to long rods or augers on the lower ends hold the structure to the ground. Steel rods may be welded onto steel plates attached to the runners for even greater strength and stability.

Fig. 8.2 show a typical runner and pier layout for a double-wide.

Set-Up

All new manufactured homes are required by HUD to have moisture barriers on the ground underneath the structure. These also function as vapor barriers. Plastic tarp materials are generally used for this purpose.

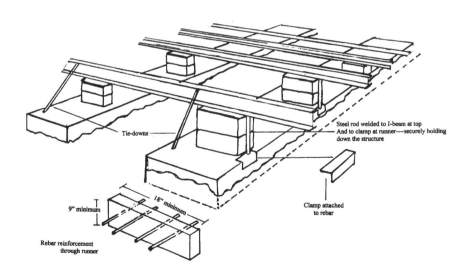

Fig. 8.3. Close-up of piers , anchoring and tie-downs.

Depending upon the ground composition, either steel rods (like those used to prevent telephone poles from leaning) are deeply driven or special augers with "shovels" are power twisted into the ground, then attached to steel straps which bolt directly to the I-beam frame.

These are called tie-downs and, when attached as recommended by HUD, will give these buildings enormous wind resistance—generally superior to most other structures.

Engineering historians agree that the Great Pyramids still remain standing after all these centuries for one fundamental reason: They're perfectly level. Those ancient engineers utilized the science of water leveling to accomplish this feat. Today, water leveling is still, by far, the most consistently accurate way to level any structure. Most manufactured homes are leveled this way. Don't allow your setup crew to use any other method.

9. Before You Buy

THERE are thousands of manufactured home dealerships in this country and it would be fruitless to attempt to make a listing of them. In Appendix A, you will find a list of each state's Manufactured Housing Association. If you wish to locate your local dealerships, and you're unsure of the manufacturer you prefer, you should write, phone or e-mail your state's association. They will provide you with all dealerships doing business within your area. They can also inform you about which manufacturers provide their products to these dealerships. Here is a list of the 25 largest U.S. manufacturers, listed in order of home production. These manufacturers will be eager to present and explain their products and assist you in finding their dealerships. Most of their websites are excellent.

Table 9.1. Contact information for the 25 biggest manufactured home manufacturers

	Company	Web Site	Phone Number
1	Champion Enterprises	www.championhomes.net	248-340-7775
2	Fleetwood Enterprises	www.fleetwoodhomes.com	909-351-3838

3	Clayton Homes	www.clayton.net	800-822-0633
4	Oakwood Homes	www.oakwoodhomes.com	336-664-4508
5	Skyline Corporation	www.skylinecorp.com	219-294-6521
6	Cavalier Homes	www.cavhomesinc.com	256-747-9800
7	Palm Harbor Homes	www.palmharbor.com	800-456-8744
8	Fairmont Homes	www.fairmonthomes.com	574-773-7941
9	Horton Homes	www.horton.com	800-657-4000
10	Patriot Homes	www.patriothomes.com	574-524-8602
11	Southern Energy Homes	www.soenergyhomes.com	877-489-3433
12	Liberty Homes	www.libertyhomes.com	800-669-8410
13	Cavco Industries	www.bikechain.com	800-950-8161
14	Four Seasons Housing	www.fourseasonshousing.com	219-825-9999
15	Pioneer Housing Systems	www.pioneerhousing.com	912-423-6630
16	Sunshine Homes	www.sunshinehomes.com	863-382-6556
17	Giles Industries	www.gilesindustries.com	877-972-3823
18	Wick Building Systems	www.wickbuildings.com	608-795-4281
19	Manufactured Housing Enterprises	www.mheinc.com	419-636-4511
20	Holly Park	www.holly-park.com	574-825-3700
21	Jacobson Homes	www.jachomes.com	800-843-1559
22	Cappaert Manufactured Homes	No website	601-636-5401
23	New Era Building Systems	www.new-era-homes.com	814-764-5581
24	Chief Industries	www.chiefind.com	492-694-5250
25	Pine Grove Manufactured Homes	www.pinegrovehomes.com	570-345-2811

How Much Do Homes Cost?

It never hurts to have a general idea as to how much a dealer should charge for a home. Prices vary from region to region and state to state. Here's a list that should keep you in the ballpark:

Table 9.2. New manufactured homes average sales price, by size of home and state for the year 2002

Region, Division and State	Average (1)	Single	Double
United States (nationwide average)	48,800	30,700	55,100
New England	55,900	42,400	57,800
Maine	48,200	33,100	66,200
New Hampshire	58,900	(S)	72,720
Vermont	43,900	(S)	50,700
Massachusetts	82,000	73,200	(S)
Rhode Island	(S)	(S)	(S)
Connecticut	(S)	(S)	(S)
Mid Atlantic	48,800	33,100	55,800
New York	49,000	34,900	54,800
New Jersey	65,400	(S)	85,900
Pennsylvania	45,800	32,200	52,200
Midwest	49,100	37,200	55,100
East North Central	48,900	32,000	54,900
Ohio	48,600	31,000	55,400
Indiana	49,200	30,500	54,400
Illinois	49,200	30,600	58,100
Michigan	49,600	33,000	53,400
Wisconsin	46,800	34,400	55,900

West North Central	49,400	33,900	55,400
Minnesota	52,100	37,900	57,900
Iowa	54,600	(S)	60,100
Missouri	45,500	29,800	52,600
North Dakota	51,100	(S)	56,100
South Dakota	56,700	(S)	59,000
Nebraska	50,000	(S)	52,600
Kansas	48,500	(S)	55,500
South	46,100	29,300	54,000
South Atlantic	48,900	29,400	54,000
Delaware	51,700	(S)	59,000
Maryland	53,800	(S)	58,800
District of Columbia	(X)	(X)	(X)
Virginia	47,000	28,100	54,700
West Virginia	45,000	28,200	51,700
North Carolina	49,500	29,200	55,300
South Carolina	50,900	31,200	55,000
Georgia	45,800	28,800	50,700
Florida	51,100	30,700	54,100
East South Central	41,700	27,400	50,500
Kentucky	41,400	26,900	51,000
Tennessee	42,600	26,500	49,700
Alabama	41,600	27,800	50,900
Mississippi	40,600	28,600	50,700
West South Central	45,100	28,200	54,300
Arkansas	40,600	28,200	51,900

Louisiana	41,400	30,100	54,000
Oklahoma	43,800	29,400	52,100
Texas	47,400	31,800	55,300
West	58,800	32,600	60,000
Mountain	53,400	32,700	57,000
Idaho	55,500	(S)	56,200
Wyoming	52,800	34,000	60,800
Colorado	57,300	32,400	62,200
New Mexico	49,400	30,500	54,800
Arizona	52,000	34,200	54,800
Utah	61,200	(S)	60,800
Nevada	55,000	(S)	56,000
Pacific	66,600	31,900	64,300
Washington	66,600	(S)	59,700
Oregon	62,200	(S)	57,600
California	68,600	(S)	68,000
Alaska	(S)	(S)	(S)
Hawaii	(S)	(S)	(S)

Legend:

(S)   Suppressed because estimate or complementary estimate based on
         fewer than five responses

(1)   Total also includes manufactured homes with more than two sections

(X)   Not Applicable

Source: These data are produced by the U.S. Commerce Department's Census
          Bureau from a survey sponsored by the Department of Housing and
          Urban Development.

What Else Will You Pay For?

To the purchase amount of the home you must also add some other items, which include:

• Transportation to your home site

• Air conditioning hookup

• Tape and texture, if ordered

• Driveway

• Ground clearing and prep

• Ground pad

• Setup and finish

• Skirting

• Well or city water hookup

• Septic tank or sewer hookup

• Electrical hookup

• Homeowner's Insurance

• Private Mortgage Insurance (PMI)

• Any additional contractor's work

If you are moving your home into a manufactured home park where you are renting your property, some of the above will be covered by the park. You will need to find out the deposit amount and total move-in cost.

The costs of these services vary greatly. So much so that a list of average prices could be misleading, so ask your sales rep to provide you with these when figuring costs.

10. Shopping For Your Home

For the best possible deal, time your shopping for the home either at the end of the month or, if possible, during the last two weeks of December (definitely the best time). Don't take this advice lightly. It can make a notable difference in the final selling price of your home, as well as improving the possibility for a person with marginal credit to obtain approval. Inventory must be moved at practically all costs and banks must sell as much money as possible.

You've compiled your resources and carefully filled out everything on your *Client Introduction Sheets*. You have your deposit or down payment funds readily available, along with your own credit reports (only if necessary. Cash buyers won't need their credit reports).

If you're a first time buyer with no credit, or if you have terrible credit (You'd better know by now), you've made arrangements with an agreeable co-applicant or buy-for who qualifies. All paperwork is gathered and ready to present. You've received all requested reports from the Better Business Bureau and weeded out the undesirable dealerships. By now you are familiar with at least a few dealerships via all those ads you've no doubt been poring over. Did you notice the numerous "phantom ads"—those describing homes that always seem to have just been sold when you inquire about them? These are used to get you onto their lots.

Practically all dealers use phantom ads, so consider these contrivances to be humorous. They're fundamentally harmless. This is truly an effective method for drumming up business.

You've called in advance and made your appointments, so you won't have to wait around for help and your sales representative will have set aside enough time to properly assist you. Buying partners have ample time to shop *together*. From examining the floor plans provided in this chapter and then filling out your *Client Introduction Sheet* in Appendix B, you should have a fairly good idea as to how you would like your new home to look and function. You either own land, you have decided on a location or you at least have a good idea as to where you would like to place this structure. You *do* know exactly how you're going to pay for your new home, right?

Now that all this preparation has armed you to the teeth, it's time to move forward. Relax and enjoy the experience of picking out your new home. Stick to the program and you'll have lots of fun with it. Just maintain two things: Lots of patience and a sense of humor.

Practically every dealership in existence uses the old "up" system. If you've neglected to set an appointment (and shame on you if you did), the sales rep greeting you is the one who was up next in line to take a customer. You're that person's "up." Salespeople are only human and are just as honest/dishonest as the customers she/he deals with every day. The line "Buyers are liars" is quite often true. Don't just automatically assume that this person is out to cheat you. By all means be perfectly honest at all times. If for any reason you feel uncomfortable with this person, request another sales rep or just leave. There is some serious business about to take place. Trust between you and the dealership is tantamount, so stay alert and be attentive to your gut feelings.

In order for your sales rep to help you choose the best home for you, she/he must know your housing wants and needs and how realistic is your ability to pay for this home. Your completely filled out *Client Introduction Sheet* will supply this person with everything she/he will need to accomplish this.

Even though most buyers feel more comfortable looking at some homes first and talking to a rep later, it's definitely better to go through the basics first. *Don't ask to look first!* A very large number of people who pull onto a sales lot are merely curiosity seekers who don't mind wasting that salesperson's time, so their reluctance to give anybody and everybody a guided tour, which will most likely net them zero, is quite understandable. They work ridiculously long hours and are usually paid straight commissions.

Just imagine how thrilled that person will be when you hand them your *Client Introduction Sheet.* You can expect their copy machines to work overtime so they can use them with future customers. No doubt, you've just made a new friend.

After all pertinent information has been supplied to your salesperson, it's time to pull out your *Apples To Apples* sheet and tour some houses.

Upon approaching the first manufactured home on the sales lot, your salesperson will go into what's called the "feature/benefit" mode. She/he will most likely begin with the exterior features, such as the I-beam frame, the siding, roofing construction and tiles, doors, potential underpinning, and so forth. After these aspects have been pointed out and their advantages explained, you will begin your indoor tour, where more features will be pointed out and their benefits further explained. For example: "This home comes with a pot-scrubber dishwasher (feature). It's called a pot-scrubber because you don't need to rinse off your dirty dishes before placing them in the dishwasher (benefit). Ms. Jones, wouldn't it be great to save all of that wasted time and energy having to scrape and rinse off all of those grungy dishes?" She/he pointed out a feature, explained its benefit, and elicited a positive response from Ms. Jones.

Just be sure to cover each and every category on your *Apples To Apples* list. Your sales rep shouldn't mind all those questions, so don't be shy.

Test closes are subtly (sometimes) used throughout the entire time you're there. For example, Ms. Jones asks the sales rep if hardwood flooring could be installed in the dining area. "Gee, Ms. Jones, I'm not really sure, but if I could talk the factory into laying hardwood floors in one of these homes, and we don't charge you extra for it, would you be seriously interested in this model?" Remember: Patience and sense of humor. Selling is a difficult and complicated process, which requires that person to have a good idea as to your desire/ability to buy one of their products. In other words, it's normal for the sales rep to "feel your pulse," so without feeling out of control, allow her/him to follow their process. Do your part and be as candid as possible.

What's the Difference Between Homes?

To establish what differences there are between different homes, carefully examine and compare the following items or areas on each of the homes you're considering:

Look at the pitch of the roof. Does it appear almost flat (3:12 pitch, most likely) or does it have a fairly steep slope (most likely a 4:12 pitch)? The steeper the pitch, the higher the cost, as well as the overall value of this home. It should be able to handle a 30 lb. load at a minimum. Ask your sales rep. Refer to the *Roofs* section of Chapter 4.

How does that roof line look? Is there a dormer added to break up the straight line? Dormers add tremendously to the aesthetic appeal of these structures. Also, dormers better facilitate the addition of porches and other structural additions. All better-made manufactured homes have at least one dormer as a part of their roof lines. Refer to the *Roofs* section of Chapter 4.

Are the roof's eaves extended very far? The best manufacturers extend theirs 12 in., which looks great, but a minimum of 4 in. will work perfectly fine. The problem with 4 in. extended eaves, though, is they cause the structure to look cheap. This detail will tell you how "upscale" this home truly is. Refer to the *Roofs* section of Chapter 4.

Is the siding Hardipanel/Maxipanel, vinyl, cedar or Smart Panel? I don't recommend Masonite, which is much cheaper and less durable. Hardipanel/Maxipanel is fire-proof, bug proof, chemical resistant, moisture resistant and practically bullet-proof. Also, homeowner's insurance can be cheaper since it is considered masonry. Vinyl siding never needs painting, requiring only being hosed down occasionally, and it is guaranteed for life. Properly maintained, cedar or split-log cedar siding is wonderfully durable. It is beautiful to look at and enhances the value of any structure. Smart-panel is coated OSB, which is extremely weather resistant. It also further increases the structural strength of the home. Refer to the *Siding* section of Chapter 4.

Look underneath at the outriggers. Do they extend all the way to the edges of the home? They should. Outriggers that don't extend to the outer perimeter of the structure don't provide enough support for the frame and will eventually allow crowning, which is the uneven settling of the structure. I would avoid any manufactured home with semi-extended outriggers. Refer to the *Flooring* section of Chapter 4.

Are those I-beams large and heavy? Ask your sales rep if they're 12 lbs. per foot in weight. The best ones are. Only the cheapest homes are built with Asian corrugated I-beams. Refer to the introductory section of Chapter 4.

Is the hitch (or are the hitches) welded on or bolted on? Bolt-ons are the best. Bolted-on hitches can be easily removed when the home is being set up and stored underneath the structure, allowing for easy skirting application at the hitch end of the structure. Welded-on hitches must be cut off with a torch and can be a sign that possibly other production short-cuts have been taken. Refer to the introductory section of Chapter 4.

Does the front entry storm door have removable glass and screening? Cheap storm doors tend to cause problems within a short period of time. A good storm door is useful and serviceable. Don't accept a flimsy door.

Does the front entry door feel solid? Does it swing in and not out? A six-panel, security entry door should be mounted here with a dead-bolt lock. It should also have a peep-hole. A quality front entry door is easily noticed and appreciated. Also, is there a door-bell mounted there?

Is the ceiling fake-textured or hand-textured? The top builders always hand texture their ceilings. Economy homes almost always have fake textured ceilings, so at least you'll know this structure was built cheaply. Refer to the *Ceilings* section of Chapter 4.

Do the walls have 1-inch battens every 8 feet? Most all manufactured homes use battens at all wall joints because these structures must move down the road before being set up, causing plaster joints to crack. There's nothing wrong with these sturdy, easily maintained walls. They're easy to keep clean because they're usually vinyl coated. However, if you've ever seen taped and textured walls in one of these homes, you'd realize that there's a legitimate reason for buying a home with standard sheetrock walls, which arrive at their setup point unpainted, and are taped, textured and painted at the setup site. It may cost more, but the difference in appearance is striking. Refer to the *Walls* section of Chapter 4.

Do the floors feel solid? That simple feel tells a lot. Thicker flooring gives less. I recommend ¾" tongue-in-groove plywood or 5/8" or thicker oriented strand board (OSB). I'd personally stay

Fig. 10.1. This kitchen has everything. (Photo courtesy Silvercrest Homes.)

clear of particle-board (Novoflor or Novadek). It doesn't hold nails well and tends to disintegrate when made wet. Refer to the *Floors* section of Chapter 4.

Are the windows dual pane and vinyl clad? It's best if they are, but storm windows work practically as well and are less costly. Single-pane windows are a clear indicator that this structure was built primarily with economy in mind, but there won't be anything economical about your heat or air conditioning bills. Refer to the *Windows* section of Chapter 4.

Are the light switches all straight or are some a little crooked? This will indicate the care of construction and attention to detail by the manufacturer.

This same examination goes for the window sills. Are they nicely detailed? Since they are normally covered by curtains or mini blinds, many shoppers have a tendency to overlook these sure-fire detail indicators.

Electrical outlets: Are there lots and lots of them or do they seem sparse? They should be no more than 6 to 8 ft. apart in the den/living/family room and in all bedrooms. Refer to the Electrical Wiring section of Chapter 4.

Are the kitchen cabinets solid wood or laminates. Anything but solid wood will eventually begin to come apart. Examine the hardware, also.

Do those upper kitchen cabinets have adjustable shelves? A small detail makes a big difference. Also, how deep are they? Many plates are 11½ inches in diameter, so the cabinets should be 12 inches deep. Refer to the *Cabinets* section of Chapter 4.

Are there tile backsplashes over the counter-tops? No good home comes without these. They should be ceramic and not plastic and they should be neatly caulked. Check out the care in detailing here.

Examine the drawers in all rooms. Are they on rollers? Do they pull in and out easily? How smooth and sturdy do they feel? If they don't run smoothly from the start, things will only get worse with use.

How good is the lighting in the kitchen? Is there any fluorescent lighting? Good lighting makes a huge difference. Are the globes glass or plastic? Once again, the use of plastic indicates that this home was built to be cheap. Plastic is bad.

Are there plastic shutoff valves underneath the sink? Although many homes have brass shutoff valves with plastic handles, which are somewhat passable, totally plastic shutoff valves *will* eventually decompose. That is what plastic does. The best shutoff valves are made completely of brass. Refer to the *Plumbing* section of Chapter 4.

Are the sinks plastic or is there plastic anywhere around the "wet" areas? There shouldn't be. Better homes have porcelain or stainless steel sinks in the kitchen and utility room, and porcelain or vitreous china sinks in the bathrooms.

Is the kitchen faucet a single-lever type? Is it metal? It should be.

Are the appliances upgraded—like a deluxe stove (It'll have a digital clock, timers, etc.), a side-by-side refrigerator/freezer with ice-maker and water dispenser, and a pot-scrubber dish washer?

How big is the water heater? A 30 gallon unit is not adequate for a home for more than 2 people. At least 40 gallons works much better. Have your sales rep show you the access panel to the water heater and look for yourself.

Is there a main water shutoff valve in the utility room? If not, find out if there's one at all. There should be one in case of a leak. Otherwise, bad things can happen. All reputable manufacturers equip their homes with main water shutoff valves. Refer to the *Plumbing* section of Chapter 4.

Is there one or even at least a couple of outside spigots. You might miss this initially, but sooner or later you'll miss having one if there isn't one. I'd recommend at least one in the back and one in the front. Refer to the *Plumbing* section of Chapter 4.

Are there electrical outlets for a clothes dryer, washer and freezer? How about a dryer vent? There is no reason for the manufacturer to expect the buyer to go through the headache of adding these items, which are so easily installed at the factory. Once again: How cheap *are* they trying to be?

How are the cabinets in the pantry and the utility room? Are they adequate? Are there any at all? How's the lighting? Fluorescent lighting is much more desirable in the utility room for many reasons. Most seem to have one tiny light fixture with a single bulb, requiring a 100 watt bulb for decent lighting. Plastic "doggie dish" light globes are a dead giveaway for a low-budget home.

While you're in there, look at the door leading outside the utility room. Is it a nice and sturdy six-panel type or is it a cheap foam-filled door? Cottage doors are also useful here, providing natural light from outside, but good security. Make sure there's a deadbolt on this door, also.

Is the main breaker in the electric service box 100 amps or 200 amps? If the home is all-electric, 200 amps are necessary. If the furnace and kitchen stove are gas, 100 amps are adequate but it's still best to go with 200 amps. The better manufacturers only install 200 amp electric service boxes in their homes. Refer to the *Electrical Wiring* section of Chapter 4.

In the bathrooms, are there two sinks in the master bathroom? Are the sinks porcelain, vitreous china or plastic? How about the tub and shower stall? Remember: Plastic is bad. The shower stall should be made of ceramic tiles or of one-piece fiberglass, not plastic, and not two-piece anything. Sooner or later, it will leak. Make sure the sinks and toilets have shutoff valves, preferably all-brass, but at least some kind of metal.

How's the tub? The nicer homes have fabulous tubs, even Jacuzzis. It should be fiberglass. Look at the fixtures. Some are made of metallic coated plastics. It's best to go with an all-metal, single-lever setup. Look for the Koehler or Moen brands. If there's a Jacuzzi tub, locate the access panel for the plumbing. It should be conveniently accessible.

How are the mirrors and lights in those baths? Are they adequate or minimal? Is that mirror just a thin piece glued to the wall? Are there dressing room lights over or around the mirror(s) in the master bath? If a full-size bathroom only has two light bulb fixtures, most likely the manufacturer is being what? That's right: cheap.

Look at the towel bars and toilet paper holders. A lot of homes lack these upon purchase, particularly in guest bathrooms. Check these to determine if they're real metal or plastic or metallic-coated plastic. Also, consider their locations for convenience.

Are there shelves in all closets and not just rods? Most better homes are supplied with "Closet Maid" shelves, which are durable, serviceable and easily replaced nation-wide. Wooden or steel rods are simply inadequate.

In the living room/den/family room, are the heating vents, windows and electrical receptacles well placed? You should always consider the placement of your furniture, especially if you have any large or oddly shaped pieces. Refer to the *AC/Heating Registers* section of Chapter 4.

Is the carpet plush or flimsy? Have your sales rep explain the brand and weight. It should be a minimum of 16 ounces and have a life-of-the-carpet warranty on the padding. A lot of people take a "barefoot tour" throughout the home. That's not a bad idea. Sculptured carpeting is generally cheaper, but it does handle wear better for a lower quality carpet. Plush carpeting is far more luxurious and costs more, but tends to wear better because of its general overall quality. It also looks considerably better. Refer to the *Carpets* section of Chapter 4.

Are mini blinds and curtains provided at no cost? They should be. You can bet that the curtains won't be of a very high quality, but most manufacturers still provide them.

Look at the trim molding at the floor and ceiling edges. Is it solid wood or laminate? Are the edges rounded? Ask if you're not sure. Fine molding adds a lot of style and value to the home and laminates are highly suspect in terms of durability. Some manufacturers also use wainscot for the lower portion of some walls. It can add a classy look. Also, chair railing is used on a lot of homes. Your own taste will determine your choice here.

How nice is the thermostat? Is it solid state and/or digital? Cheap, non-digital thermostats have a tendency to be inaccurate and can cost you in utility bills. Ask your sales rep. They shouldn't have a problem replacing a $5.00 thermostat with one that costs $30.00 in order to make a sale.

It is rare that someone finds a home with all amenities perfectly suitable to their needs and desires. Most everything in a home can be upgraded later. I have indicated how to pretty much look for a perfect home, but that home might not be found, but rather developed, so look at the potential just as much as for what's before you. Practically everything I mentioned here can be ordered as an option. For this reason, many manufactured home buyers choose to custom order their homes, which should only cost slightly more than buying one "off the lot." If it does cost more, the difference should be nominal.

You should also keep in mind that a large number of manufactured home buyers are looking for basic, inexpensive housing, so the use of various low-cost materials enables them to fit the purchase of these homes into their budgets.

Quite a lot of money can be saved by omitting certain items, which you can buy from a home supply store. Ceiling fans can cost you less than having the factory install them. Just be sure to have all pertinent light fixtures braced and wired at the factory, which costs very little. Then, you can easily install much nicer fixtures at a lower cost.

It's OK for the factory to install phone jacks, computer and cable connections, just as long as they're located where you want them. Otherwise, have these installed by your own contractor.

You should not make any type of buying decision until you've shopped all of the dealerships you've chosen to visit, and not until all of your *Apples To Apples* sheets have been fully filled out and carefully compared.

A sales manager, or at least another salesperson, may be introduced to you so she/he can further assist you in making some sort of buying decision. In sales terms this is called a "T.O.," meaning to turn over to another sales closer. That's OK. It's their job. Leave with a smile. Tell them you'll be in touch really soon and go on to your next appointment.

Good salespeople make follow-up calls. That's OK, too. Give them the chance to earn your business. Their job is to dangle the best possible carrot in front of you. Yours is simply to allow them to do *just that*! Merely the knowledge that you're "shopping" them can steer this dealership in the direction of giving you an even better deal. Some people have a tendency to get caught up into the "ether" and go along with the rush. We know better, though, so stick to the program.

You shouldn't expect to leave with any firm asking prices for the homes you just examined. Even if they do throw some prices at you, just take them with a grain of salt. Ball-park figures are all you should expect at this juncture, so don't feel insulted or get angry with them for appearing vague about their prices. Visit number two (if they've earned it) will draw this out of them.

Visit two or three more dealerships and no more, unless you still haven't found the right home. Almost any dealer can find the proper home for you if they're willing to invest the time and effort to do so. Unless you're extremely precise about what you want, three dealerships should be plenty.

And The Winner Is...

Assuming you've stuck to the program and completed all of your appointments, narrowing down to your one or two "favorites" should be a snap. Your *Apples To Apples* sheet should supply you with most, if not all the information you'll need to determine who'll remain in the running.

Set appointment-number two with the pertinent dealers. Make note of any questions you have. With *Apples To Apples* sheet in hand, go through each remaining prospective home with a fine-toothed comb. At this point you should expect all claims to be put in writing. Stay on top of your notes and make certain all questions are answered.

Whether you're considering a home already on the lot, or if you plan to order your home from the factory, their prices are too similar to make a big difference. The only exception would be a home that has been on the lot for 12 months or longer. A dealer should be losing money on this unit, so any reasonable offer should be quickly accepted. This principle applies to some, but certainly not all repossessed units. They can be liabilities to these dealers and they'll oftentimes be willing to "lose" money just to get rid of them. Repos aren't generally the bargain most would imagine, since the lender must recover all of the funds it loaned out to the initial purchaser.

It's generally better to look for bargains on new homes.

Whether or not you have narrowed your choices down to one, two or even three homes, the dealers don't need to know all the details. The key to obtaining the best deal on your new home is creating competition among these dealers for your business. Also, unless the sales manager is seriously involved, the price can probably go down a bit. No one will offer the best price right up front. No dealer should expect to stay in business by just giving homes away to everyone. Plus, lenders do not allow dealers to sell their homes over a certain percentage over invoice, so they actually *can't* rip you off price-wise.

Don't make your final decision until you've gotten the "best shot" from each dealer. Make it a point to arrive at your final decision at *your* home, not theirs. Even if you do end up buying that particular home, many years of payments and upkeep logically shouldn't be decided by one conversation. Once you've decided upon your new home, and only then, you may fill out a credit application with them (once again, if you're not paying cash). You will then have to wait one day to a couple of weeks to hear back from the lender(s). Once your financing has been approved and your loan figures are in front of you, you must thoroughly go over the purchase agreement with them (they *all* have purchase agreements). Ask for a written time frame for all promised services and all names and numbers of the companies and individuals performing these services. Once you're awaiting delivery and services, you'll understand why doing this is so absolutely crucial. They must also give you a written time frame for skirting and deck building appointments, appliance and furniture deliveries and whatever else is to be done after setup. Be fair and reasonable with them, but you need a solid commitment. Make it perfectly clear that they will receive your monetary commitment (down payment or deposit) only after both parties have signed a purchase agreement containing everything you've been promised, and both parties possess a copy of this agreement. If they refuse to comply, walk. No respectable business will sell a high-ticket item and its services without everything spelled out in writing. "If it ain't in writing', it ain't."

Only after everything is in order should you give them your deposit or down payment. *Never before!* Do not give a dealer any money you don't intend to get back. Pay by check *only*. They must issue you a receipt, which states that your money must be refunded within two weeks upon demand, unless you've ordered your home or created other expenses. Then you've relinquished either some or all of it.

11. The Closing

YOU'VE chosen your home, carefully negotiated and signed your purchase agreement, forked over your down payment and received approval from your lender with each and every condition met (non-cash purchasers, only). If you ordered your home from the factory it must have arrived and is sitting on the lot. Do not proceed if you've not yet inspected your home. Bad things can happen, otherwise. The next step is to sign all of the pertinent legal documents and assume responsibility for your loan and your new home.

Your dealer will set up a specific time for all participating parties to gather for *The Closing*. This will require the presence of your co-signer or buy-for friend, if needed. Upon your arrival the manager or sales rep should walk you through your home in order to familiarize you with its features as well as the servicing and setup aspects of the structure. Then you will all be seated around a table, the door will be closed and you will proceed to spend the next hour or so reading and signing each of the legal documents required for the closure of this sale. These will include:

An arbitration agreement to which you agree that, in case of a future dispute between the buyer and the seller, an independently chosen arbitrator, normally a judge or an attorney, will settle your disagreement in a fair and unbiased manner without resorting to a legal suit. This is done in all cases and should, by all means, be signed. Historically, legal arbitrators have tended to lean toward the rights of the buyers of manufactured homes.

• All lenders documents

• Warranties

• Insurance papers

• Any and all service agreements

• All waivers

• Statements involving responsibilities (promises) of the buyer, seller or both

Once these documents have all been signed, you will then review everything you have just discussed and signed. A lot of dealers tape record this review, which is a terrific idea. This protects both parties from future misunderstandings. Don't leave until you are perfectly clear about everything you wish to have clarified.

Also, it is the responsibility of the new manufactured home owner to acquire a homeowner's insurance policy for their home. This protects the investment for both parties and is always necessary in order for the lender to fund the transaction. These are always offered at the closing. Refusing to purchase homeowners insurance will void the deal and you will leave without having acquired your new home. For this reason, it is only reasonable to suggest that you contact a few insurance agents for policy information and quotes for their policies well before the closing occurs. You may find better rates and coverage.

Most lenders also require private mortgage insurance (PMI), which insures that the house will be paid off in full in case of the buyer's death. One or both types of insurance can be added to your loan amount, so your mortgage payments, and possibly your interest rates, will increase, so don't neglect to leave this additional $60.00 to $70.00 off your monthly budget.

When the closing session has ended, if you paid cash for this home, it's now yours. However, if you're financing your home, the final portion of the closing is your phone audit. Once your home has been set up, you must contact your lender to answer questions verifying exactly what you've purchased and received with their loan. A phone audit is necessary for the lender to make sure the dealer isn't cheating them out of items such as furniture or appliances or other extras they may have received money for without providing them to the buyer. Lying to your lender is bank fraud, which is a federal felony offense. If your dealer suggests bending the truth, don't *even* think about it. Properly answer each and every question you are asked. Don't hide anything.

During the next couple of weeks the quality of the service provided by your dealer will reveal itself. You've been provided with a checklist for when your home is being set up. Keeping up with this list will provide you with excellent documentation as to the condition of your home upon arrival, how well it was set up and how timely corrections were made. Fill out this check-list properly and completely.

If, even after you've tried to avoid problems, it becomes obvious that your service was not up to par, do your duty and fill out a complaint with the Better Business Bureau. But, do make certain that you have given this dealer every reasonable opportunity to resolve your problem. Be sure they truly intended to either do you right or cheat you. If this dealership actually managed to hoodwink you, it should be possible to remove them. But, if you are truly satisfied

Fig. 11.1. Two house sections on the lot, before set-up.

with your home and the service which was provided by your dealer, make sure to refer these "good guys" to anyone you come across who may be interested in purchasing a manufactured home. Most dealers award individuals anywhere from $100.00 to $500.00 for referring customers who buy a home from them. You can bet they'll let you know this if they do.

There may not be a precise formula for success, but adhering to logically thought-out guidelines is normally necessary to avoid the most common pitfalls. It's possible that you may visit just one dealership, pick out a home right then and there, blindly follow their advice and come out smelling like a rose—but, seriously, what are the odds?

If you have thoroughly read this book and utilize the tools it provides, you should be ahead of the game and a delight for most sales reps to work with. You should succeed in intelligently choosing and purchasing a home that meets or exceeds your expectations. You'll know that you haven't approached this important endeavor blindly and, hey, you just might have a lot of fun with it.

Happy home hunting!

12. Customizing Your Home

A S I TRAVELED across the country, I became delighted at the ingenuity and creativity of so many owners of manufactured homes. I couldn't possibly count the times I've scratched my head, trying to figure out if the structure I was admiring was a site-built home or if it was indeed manufactured.

Since manufactured homes are fundamentally built just the same as site-built homes, there's absolutely no problem building additions on to the structures. Most common among these addi-

Fig. 121. The super low-budget solution: two single-wides connected.

Above: Fig. 12.2. A tastefully appointed single-wide.

tions are the attachment of decks and porches. The second most common is the addition of carports. Other add-ons include garages, extended roofs, decking around swimming pools, large dens or recreation rooms, workshops and breezeways leading to other structures such as barns, stables and even larger structures such as indoor riding arenas. While in Texas, I even saw an airplane

Below: Fig. 12.3. Rear deck on tastefully appointed singe-wide.

Fig. 12.4. Two single-wides connected with a garden porch attached.

hangar that had siding and trim that matched the adjacent triple-wide, garage and barn.

Manufactured homes are constructed of commonly found materials, so matching siding, roofing, flooring and other items, such as windows and gutters, is a relatively simple task. About the only non-standard items (and only on some manufactured homes) are the dimensions of some doors. This can be evened out by either enlarging the door-frames on the existing structure, or by utilizing

Fig. 12.5. Older single-wide with large room built on.

119

Fig. 12.6. Front and side porches built on.

doors equal in size to the original ones. I would normally recommend the former.

Windows and doors can be added virtually anywhere desired, so additions such as sliding glass doors, bay windows or just about anything else, are simple to do.

Even though your manufactured home will be sitting on piers, an alternative foundation for the adjoining structure is just fine. Many additions sit upon solid concrete slabs, while others may sit on piers or, like a barn, a pole-type structure.

Fig. 12.7. Matching workshop building.

Further enhancements to your home can come by way of creative landscaping and via the use of a matching, unattached structure, such as a gazebo, an arbor, an in-ground or decked above-ground swimming pool, a shop, playhouse, garage, or carport.

In addition to these normal add-ons, some innovative owners of manufactured homes have actually dug basements or cellars and have even (with structural reinforcement, of course) added a second story to the house.

Above: Fig. 12.8. Porch and room additions.

Below: Fig. 12.9. Simple carport attached to the side of the home.

Fig. 12.10. Added-on screened porch.

It's not at all uncommon to find single-wides that have been re-roofed and sided in a such a manner that it's next to impossible to tell it's not a standard site-built home. Attaching two or more single-wides together has produced some rather remarkable results. Numerous innovative individuals have created absolutely wonderful homes, which are virtually indistinguishable from site-built ones, for literally just a few thousand dollars!

While working for a dealership in Austin, Texas, I had the pleasure of assisting an innovative couple, who ordered a double-wide blue nailed (see Chapter 4) and set it up on a large, picturesque piece of property overlooking a lake. They provided their own roofing materials, siding, decking, all kitchen and bathroom tiles and all of their flooring. They added on a three-car garage and a

Fig. 12.11. Wraparound porch and extended roof and pool deck.

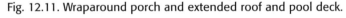

Above: Fig. 12.12. Note the matching pitch on the outbuilding roof.

Below: Fig. 12.13. Back deck and utility room porch.

splendidly decked swimming pool, and they also had built a matching garage and horse barn. The results were astounding! The best part is it cost them about half of what it would had they chosen to go with a standard site-built home.

It's been said that "a picture says a thousand words," so I've included the photos of some homes which have been enhanced by their creative owners. These will probably give you some ideas of what has been achieved and how that can be done. And perhaps you can come up with a few ideas of your own. The sky's the limit, so have fun with it.

Appendix A: Getting Help with Your Manufactured Home

IN ORDER for the manufactured home shopper to acquire a listing of the manufacturers and/or dealerships doing business in their area or state, or for the buyer to assure fair treatment or enforcement of the law pertaining to the purchase, setup or servicing of a new home, it is sometimes necessary to contact their state's "powers-that-be" and information providers or, in some instances, HUD's national office. Each state, with the exceptions of Alaska, Hawaii, Rhode Island and Wisconsin, has an association, which oversees the ways and means of the dealerships and manufacturers within their prospective states, and some states have maybe just one or the other. Listed underneath each state's manufactured housing association you will see the information for their respective state administrative agencies.

There are, however, 13 states that don't have their own State Agency responsible for manufactured housing. If you live in one of those 13 states (Alaska, Connecticut, Delaware, Hawaii, Kansas, Massachusetts, Montana, New Hampshire, North Dakota, Ohio, Oklahoma, Vermont, and West Virginia), you will have to contact the federal office for HUD for enforcement:

U.S. Department of Housing and Urban Development
451 7th Street, SW
Washington, DC 20410
Tel.:   1-800-927-2891
E-mail: mhs@hud.gov
Other phone numbers:
(202) 708-1112
TTY: (202) 708-1455

Whichever agency or association you contact, always provide the following information:

- Your name, address and a telephone number where you can be reached during the day;

- The name of the manufacturer;

- Serial number and model number of your manufactured home;

- Label number (on the red tag on the back of the home);

- The date you purchased the home;

- The name and address of the retailer from whom you purchased the home;

- A description of the problem;

- Copies of any correspondence or contracts with the retailer and the manufacturer, documenting your attempts to resolve the problem.

Alabama

Alabama Manufactured Housing Institute
Sherry Norris, Executive Director
4274 Lomac St.
Montgomery, AL 36106

Tel.: 334-244-7828, Ext. 22
Fax: 334-244-9339
E-mail: amhi.nor@mindspring.com

State Agency:

Manufactured Housing Commission
906 South Hull St.
Montgomery, AL 36130

Alaska

There is no manufactured housing institute in this state

State Agency:

None (Contact National HUD Office)

Arizona

Manufactured Housing Industry of Arizona
Mr. Grub Mix, Executive Director
PO Box 24049
Tempe, AZ 85265

Tel.: 602-456-6530
Fax, 602-966-9776
E-mail: info@mhiaz.org

State Agency:

Department of Building and Fire Safety
Office of Manufactured Housing
1540 West Van Buren
Phoenix, AZ 85007

Arkansas

Arkansas Manufactured Housing
Association
Mr. J.D. Harper, Executive Director
2500 McCain Place, Suite 203
N. Little Rock, AR 72116

E-mail: harper@amha.net

State Agency:

Arkansas Manufactured Home
Commission
523 South Louisiana St. Suite 500,
Lafayette Bldg.
Little Rock, AR 72201

California

California Manufactured Housing
Institute
Mr. Robert N. West
10630 Town Center Drive, Suite 120
Rancho Cucamonga, CA 91730

Tel.: 909-987-2599
Fax: 909-989-0434
E-Mail:
mcm.att.net@worldnet.att.net

Western Mobilehome Parkowners
Ass. (WMA)
1007 7th Street, Suite 300
Sacramento, CA 95814

Tel.: 916-448-7002
Fax: 916-448-7085
E-mail: sheila@wma.org

California Mobilehome Parkowners
Alliance
Ms. Chelu Travesco, VP
1801 E. Edinger Ave, Suite No. 230
Santa Ana, CA 92705

Tel.: 714-480-1137
Fax: 714-480-1137
E-mail: mcm.att.net@worldnet.net

State Agency:

Department of Housing and
Community Development

Division of Codes and Standards,
Manufactured Housing Section
PO Box 31
Sacramento, CA 95812-0031

Colorado

Colorado Manufactured Housing
Association
Ms. Bonnie Geiger, Executive
Director
1410 Grant St., Suite D-110
Denver, CO 80203

Tel.: 303-832-2022
Fax: 303-830-0826
E-mail: coloradohomes.org

State Agency:

Housing Division, Department of
Local Affairs
1313 Sherman Street, No. 323
Denver CO 80203

Connecticut

Connecticut Manufactured Housing
Association
Mr. Joseph Mike
PO Box 605
Bristol, CT 06011-0605

Tel.: 860-584-5915
Fax: 860-584-5930
E-mail: tompreato@snet.net

State Agency:

None (Contact National HUD Office)

Delaware

First State Manufactured Housing
Association
Ms. Phyllis Mckinley, Executive
Director
PO Box 1829
Dover DE 19903

Tel.: 302-674-5868
Fax: 302-674-5960
E-mail: phyllis@firstatema.org

State Agency:

None (Contact National HUD Office)

Florida

Florida Manufactured Housing Association
Mr. Frank Williams, Executive Director
115 North Calhoun, Suite 5
Tallahassee, FL 32301

Tel.: 850-907-9111
Fax: 850-907-9119
E-mail: fmha@nettally.com

State Agency:

Bureau of Mobile Homes and R.V.,
Division of Motor vehicles
2900 Apalachee Pkwy., Room A-129
Talahassee, FL 32399-0640

Georgia

Georgia Manufactured Housing Association
Ms. Charlotte Gattis, Executive Director
1000 Circle 75 Parkway, #600
Atlanta, GA 30339

Tel.: 770-955-4522
Fax: 770-955-5575
E-mail: info@gmha.com

State Agency:

Manufactured Housing Division,
State Fire Marshall's Office
2 Martin Luther King, Jr. Drive
Atlanta, GA 30334

Hawaii

There is no manufactured housing institute in this state.

State Agency:

None (Contact National HUD Office)

Idaho

Idaho Manufactured Housing Association
Mr. Grub Mix, Executive Director
PO Box 201
Sun Valley, ID 83353

Tel.: 208-343-1722
Fax: 208-622-6523
E-mail: gmxmhs@aol.com

State Agency:

Buildings Division, Department of Labor and Industrial Services
277 North Sixth Street, Statehouse Mall
Boise, ID 83720
Illinois

Illinois Manufactured Housing Association
Mike Marlowe, Executive Director
3888 Peoria Rd.
Springfield, IL 62702

Tel.: 217-528-3423
Fax: 217-544-4642
E-mail: mhrv@lcys.net

State Agency:

None (Contact National HUD Office)

Indiana

Indiana Manufactured Housing Association
Mr. Dennis Harney, Executive Vice President
3210 Rand Road
Indianapolis, IN 50316

Tel.: 317-247-6258
Fax: 317-243-9174
E-mail: imharavic@ix.netcom.net

State Agency:

Codes Enforcement Division, Dept. of Fire Prevention & Bldg. Svcs.
402 West Washington St., Room W-246
Indianapolis, IN 46204

Iowa

Manufactured Housing Association of Iowa
Mr. Joe Kelly, Executive Vice President
1400 Dean Avenue
Des Moines, IA 50316

Tel.: 515-265-1497
Fax: 515-265-6480
E-mail: house@netins.net

State Agency:

Iowa State Building Code Bureau
Department of Public Safety
Wallace State Office Building
Des Moines, IA 50319-0047

Kansas

Kansas Manufactured Housing Association
Ms. Martha Neu Smith, Executive Director
214 SW 6th Street, Suite 206
Topeka, KS 66603-3719

Tel.: 913-357-5256
Fax: 913-357-5257
E-mail: kmhal@mindspring.com

State Agency:

None (Contact National HUD Office)

Kentucky

Kentucky Manufactured Housing Institute
Mr. Thad I. Vann, Executive Director
2170 US 127 South
Frankfort, KY 40601

Tel.: 502-223-0490
Fax: 502-223-7305
E-mail: kmhi@dcr.net

State Agency:

Manufactured Housing Division
Department of Housing, Building and Construction

1047 U.S. 127, South Building
Frankfort, KY 40601

Louisiana

Louisiana Manufactured Housing Association
Mr. Steve Duke, Executive Director
4847 Revere Avenue
Baton Rouge, LA 70808

Tel.: 504-925-9041
Fax: 504-925-1208
E-mail: steve@1mha.com

State Agency:

Manufactured Housing Division,
State Fire Marshall's Office
5150 Florida Boulevard
Baton Rouge, LA 70806

Maine

Manufactured Housing Association of Maine
Ms. Karen Brown-Mohr, Executive Director
3 Wade Street, Lescomb Building
Augusta, ME 04330

Tel.: 207-623-4221
Fax: 207-622-4437
E-mail: kbrownmohr@worldnetatt.net

State Agency:

Manufactured Housing Board
Department of Professional and Financial Regulation
State House, Station 35
Augusta, ME 04333

Maryland

Manufactured Housing Institute of Maryland, Inc.
Mr. Lowell Cochran, Executive Director
PO Box 1158
Hagerstown, MD 21740-1158

Tel.: 301-797-5341
Fax: 301-797-6836
E-mail: mhiomf@aol.com

State Agency:

Department of Housing and
Community Development, Maryland
Code Administration
100 Community Place
Crownsville, MD 21032-2023

Massachusetts

Massachusetts Manufactured
Housing Association
Mr. Richard B. Morton, Exec.
Director
PO Box 5963
Marlborough, MA 01752

Tel.: 508-460-9523
Fax: 508-460-9361
E-mail: mhrv@lcys.net

State Agency:

None (Contact National HUD Office)

Michigan

Michigan Manufactured Housing
Association
Mr. Tim DeWitt, Executive Director
2222 Association Dr.
Okemos, ME 44864-5978

Tel.: 517-349-3300
Fax: 517-349-3543
E-mail: tdwitt@mmhrvca.org

State Agency:

Manufactured Housing and Land
Resources Division
Corporation and Securities Bureau
PO Box 30222
Lansing, MI 489909

Minnesota

Minnesota Manufactured Housing
Association

Mr. Mark Brunner, Executive Vice
President
1540 Humboldt Ave., Suite 205
West St. Paul, MN 55118

Tel.: 651-450-4700
Fax: 651-450-1111
E-mail: evpmail@mnmfghome.org

State Agency:

Manufactured Housing Structures
Section
Building Codes and Standards
Division, Department of
Administration
498 Metro Square Building
St. Paul, MN 35101

Mississippi

Mississippi Manufactured Housing
Association
Ms. Jennifer Hall, Executive Director
PO Box 54266
Pearl, MS 39288-4266

Tel.: 601-939-8820
Fax: 601-939-7988
E-Mail: jenhall@msmmha.com

State Agency:

Mobile Home Inspection Division
Office of the Fire Marshall
PO Box 22542
Jackson, MS 39205-2542

Missouri

Missouri Manufactured Housing
Association
Ms. Joyce Baker, Executive Director
PO Box 1365
4748 Country Club Drive
Jefferson City, MO 65102

Tel.: 314-636-8660
Fax: 314-636-4912
E-Mail: mmha@socket.net

State Agency:

Dept. of Manufactured Housing, R.V.
& Modular Units
Public Service Commission
PO Box 360
Jefferson City, MO 65102

Montana

Montana Manufactured Housing
Association
Mr. Stuart Doggett, Executive
Director
7 West 6th Avenue, Suite 507
Helena, MT 59601

Tel.: 406-442-2164
Fax: 406-442-8018
E-Mail: stiart@initco/net

State Agency:

None (Contact National HUD Office)

Nebraska

Nebraska Manufactured Housing
Institute, Inc.
Mr. Martin Huff, Executive Director
5300 West O Street
Lincoln, NE 68528

Tel.: 402-475-3675
Fax: 702-737-0299
E-Mail: nemanufacturedhomes.com

State Agency:

Division of Housing and Recreational
Vehicles
Department of Health
PO Box 95007
Lincoln, NE 68509-5007

Nevada

Nevada Manufactured Housing
Association
Mr. Grub Mix, Executive Director

3160 E. Desert Inn Road #3-165
Las Vegas, NV 89121

Tel.: 702-737-7778
Fax: 702-737-0299
E-mail: gmixmhs@aol.com

State Agency:

Nevada Department of Commerce
Manufactured Housing Division
2601 E. Sahara Ave. Suite 259
Los Vegas, NV 89104

New Hampshire

New Hampshire Manufactured
Housing Association
Ms. Jodi Grimbilas, Executive
Director
P.O. Box 451
Concord, NH 03302-0163

Tel.: 603-225-7170
Fax: 603-226-0165
E-mail: mhrv@lcsys.net

State Agency:

None (Contact National HUD Office)

New Jersey

New Jersey Manufactured Housing
Association
Ms. Judith A Thornton, Executive
Director
2382 Whitehorse-Mercerville Road
Trenton, NJ 08619

Tel.: 609-588-9040
Fax: 609-588-9041
E-Mail: njmha@njmha.org

State Agency:

Division of Housing And
Development, Bureau of Code
Services
3131 Princeton Pike, CN 816
Trenton, NJ 08625-0816

New Mexico

New Mexico Manufactured Housing Association
Mr. Mark Duran, Executive director
6400 Uptown Blvd.
Albuquerque, NM 87110

Tel.: 505-830-3764
Fax: 505-830-3772
E-Mail:nmmha@nmmha.com

State Agency:

Manufactured Housing Division
Regulation & Licensing Department
725 St. Michael's Drive
PO Box 25101
Santa Fe, NM 87504

New York

New York Manufactured Housing Association
Ms. Nancy Geer, Executive Director
421 New Karner Road
Albany, NY 12205-3809

Tel.: 518-464-5087 or 800-721-HOME
Fax: 518-464-5096
E-Mail: info@nymha.org

State Agency:

Housing and Building Codes Bureau
Division of Housing and Community Renewal
One Fordham Plaza, Room S-356
Bronx, NY 10458

North Carolina

North Carolina Manufactured Housing Institute
Mr. Steve Zamiara, Executive Director
PO Box 58648
Raleigh, NC 27658-8648

Tel.: 919-872-2740
Fax: 919-872-4826
E-Mail: stevez@ncmhi.com

State Agency:

Manufactured Housing Division
Department of Insurance
PO Box 26387
Raleigh, NC 27611

North Dakota

North Dakota Manufactured Housing Association
Mr. Shayne Walth, Certified Representative
PO Box 2681
Bismark, ND 58502

Tel.: 701-667-2187
Fax: 701-667-2187
E-Mail: ndmha@btigate.com

State Agency:

None (Contact National HUD Office)

Ohio

Ohio Manufactured Housing Association
Mr. Tim Williams, Executive Vice President
201 Bradenton Ave., Suite 100
Dublin, OH 43017

Tel.: 614-799-2340
Fax: 614-799-0616
E-Mail: hfo@homesforohio.org

State Agency:

None (Contact National HUD Office)

Oklahoma

Manufactured Housing Association of Oklahoma
Ms. Deanna Fields, Executive Director
PO Box 32309
Oklahoma City, OK 73123

Tel.: 405-634-5050 or 00-242-7642
Fax: 405-634-5355
E-mail: mhao@mhao.org

State Agency:

None (Contact National HUD Office)

Oregon

Manufactured Housing Commuities of Oregon
Mr. Chuck Carpenter, Executive director
3847 Woverine St. NE, Suite 22
Salem, OR 97305

Tel.: 800-488-6426
Fax: 503-391-4652
E-Mail: mhcocc@uswest.net

State Agency:

Building Codes Division
Department of Consumer and
Business Services
1535 Edgewater Drive, NW
Salem, OR 97310

Pennsylvania

Pennsylvania Manufactured Housing
Association
Ms. Mary Gaiski, Executive Vice
President
PO Box 248, Routes 114 & I-83
New Cumberland, PA 17070

Tel.: 717-774-3440
Fax: 717-774-5596
E-Mail: general@pmha.org

State Agency:

Division of Manufactured Housing
Department of Community Affairs
Forum Building, No. 376
Harrisburg, PA 17120

Rhode Island

There is no manufactured housing
institute in this state

State Agency:

Building Code Commission
Department of Administration
One Capitol Hill
Providence, RI 02908-5859

South Carolina

Manufactured Housing Institute of
South Carolina
Mr. Mark Dillard, Executive Director
PO Box 1781
Columbia, SC 29202

Tel.: 803-771-9046
Fax: 803-771-7023
E-mail: mhisc@mhisc.com

State Agency:

SC Department of Labor, Licensing &
Regulation
Building & Related Services
3600 Forest Drive, PO Box 11329
Columbia, SC 29211-1329

South Dakota

South Dakota Manufactured Housing
Association
Mr. Jerry L. Vogeler, Executive
Director
PO Box 7077
Pierre, SD 57501-7077

Tel.: 605-223-2065 or 800-765-4352
Fax: 605-223-2061
E-Mail:jerryvogeler@pie.midco.net

State Agency:

Commercial Inspection and
Regulation Division
Department of Commerce and
Regulation
118 West Capitol Avenue
Pierre, SD 57501-5070

Tennessee

Tennessee Manufactured Housing
Association
Ms. Bonita Hamm, Executive
Director
240 Great Circle Road, Suite 332
Nashville, TN 37228

Tel.: 615-256-4733
Fax: 615-255-8869
E-Mail: tmha@bellsouth.net

State Agency:

Manufactured Housing Section
Division of Fire Prevention, 3rd Floor
500 James Robertson Parkway
Nashville, TN 37243-1160

Texas

Texas Manufactured Housing
Association
Ms. Jody Anderson, Interim
President
8105 Exchange Drive
PO Box 141429
Austin, TX 78714

Tel.: 512-459-1222
Fax: 512-459-1511
E-Mail: mhrv@lcsys.net

State Agency:

Manufactured Housing Division
Department of Licensing and
Regulations
PO Box 12157, Capitol Station
Austin, TX 78711

Utah

Utah Manufactured Housing
Association
Mr. Gub Mix, Executive Director
329 Juniper Road
Sun Valley, ID 83353

Tel.: 208-343-1722
Fax: 208-622-6523
E-mail: gmixmhs@aol.com

State Agency:

Division of Occupational and
Professional Licensing
Department of Commerce
PO Box 45805
Salt Lake City, UT 84145-0805

Vermont

Vermont Manufactured Housing
Association
89 Roosevelt Highway
Colchester, VT 05446

Tel.: 802-872-5808
Fax: 802-879-7710

State Agency:

None (Contact National HUD Office)

Virginia

Virginia Manufactured Housing
Association
Mr. Ron Dunlap, Executive Director
8413 Patterson Avenue
Richmond, VA 23229

Tel.: 804-750-2500
Fax: 804-741-3027
E-Mail: rdunlap@vamha.com

State Agency:

Manufactured Housing Office
Dept. of Housing & Community
Development
Jackson Center, 501 N. Second St.
Richmond, VA 23219-1321

Washington

Washington Manufactured Housing
Association
Ken Spencer, Executive director
Manufactured Housing Communities
of Washington, Inc.
1530 Evergreen Park Drive SW
Olympia, WA 98502

Tel.: 360-357-5650
Fax: 360-357-5651
E-mail: wmha@worldnet.att.net

State Agency:

Office of Manufactured Housing
Dept. Of Community Trade &
Economic Development
PO Box 48300, 906 Columbia St. SW
Olympia, WA 98504-8300

West Virginia

West Virginia Manufactured Housing
Association
Mr. Jeff Moore, Executive Director
205 First Avenue
Nitro, WV 25143

Tel.: 304-727-7431
Fax: 304-727-1172
E-Mail: wvasoff@newwave.net

State Agency:

West Virginia Division of Labor
319 Building Three, Capitol Complex
Charleston, WV 25305

Wisconsin

There is no manufactured housing
institute in this state

State Agency:

Manufactured Homes, Safety &
Building Division
PO Box 7969
Madison, WI 53707

Wyoming

Wyoming Manufactured Housing
Association
Laurie Urbiqkit, Executive Director
PO Box 1493 Riverton, WY 82501

Tel.: 307-857-6001
Fax: 307-857-0537
E-Mail: l@wyoming.com

State Agency:

None (Contact National HUD Office)

Appendix B: Checklists and Charts

Table 1. Home Buyer's Information

Name
Current Address
Home Phone: Work Phone: Other:
Occupation:
Reason for Moving:
How many to live in new home: Ages:
Present Dwelling: House Manufactured Home Apartment Other
Housing Situation: Own Outright Purchasing Rent or Lease Other
Current Rent or Mortgage Payment: $ per month or $ per
If mortgaged, how much is owned? $
How long at current residence?
Reason for considering a manufactured home:
Manufactured Home Desired: Single-wide Double-wide Triple-wide
Home Placement: I have my own land I wish to buy land I wish to purchase a lot
In a sub-division I am interested in leasing property in a manufactured home community
I have a manufactured home as a trade-in: Yes No
I own my trade-in outright: Yes No— currently owe $
Year of trade-in: Manufacturer of trade-in:
My trade-in is a single-wide double-wide triple-wide No. bedrooms: No. baths:
I plan to move into my home on or by:
I will pay cash I am financing my home only I wish to finance both land and home
Institution financing my home:
I will need your assistance in financing this transaction Yes No Please advise

Table 1, continued

On my credit score my Beacon score is:	and/or my Empirica score is:
I (we) will pay no more than $ cash or $	down payment and $ /mo
I (we) am (are) interested in purchasing furnishing for the home: Yes No	
Number and description of bedrooms desired:	
Number and description of bathrooms desired:	
Other features desired:	

Table 2. Apples to Apples

2.a. General Information

Dealer:	Sales representative:
Phone Number:	Appointment time:
Home Manufacturer:	Model number:
Manufacture Date:	Retail price:
New Used Single-wide	Double-wide Triple-wide
Home will be delivered by (Company Name):	
Contact Person:	Phone number:
Home will be serviced by (Company Name):	
Contact Person:	Phone number:
Dealership rating:	Excellent Good Fair Poor

2.b. Substructure

Frame (I-Beams): USA Steel	Asian Corrugated Steel
Outriggers: Fully Extended	Partially Extended
Hitch(es): Removable (bolted on)	Welded to the frame

136

2.c. Exterior

Siding:	Smart Panel		Hardipanel (Maxipanel)
	Vinyl	Cedar	Masonite
		Other	
Roof Covering:	Shingles	Steel	Aluminum
	Other (describe):		

2.d. Main Structure

Wall Sheathing:	OSB	Plywood	None
Roof Decking:	OSB		Plywood
Exterior Wall Studs:	2 X 6, 16 in. OC		2 X 4, 16 in. OC
	2 X 4, 24 in. OC		2 X 3, 16 in. OC
		2 X 3, 2 in. OC	
Sheetrock thickness:	$5/8$ in.	$3/4$ in.	$3/8$ in.
Roof Structure:	2 X 4, 16 in. OC trusses		2 X 4, 24 in. OC trusses
	2 X 2, 16 in. OC birdcage		2 X 4, 24 in. OC birdcage
	Hinged w/ 2 X 4 trusses		Other:
Steel straps/exterior wall studs to floor:	Yes		No
Steel straps/exterior wall studs to roof	Yes		No
Roof overhang length:	Inches		
Windows:	Thermopane	Storm	Single pane

2.e. Floors

Joists:	2 X 8, 16 in. OC	2 X 6, 16 in. OC	2 X 6, 24 in. OC
	2 X 4, 16 in. OC	2 X 4, 24 in. OC	Other:
Floor decking:	OSB		¾ in. Tongue-in groove plywood
	Other Plywood		Particle board
Wet area flooring	OSB	Plywood	Other
Carpeting:	Ounces	Plush	Sculptured
Warranty:			
Carpet pad:	Rebond	Foam	Warranty:
Ceiling texturing:	Hand textured		Molded (fake)
Insulation:	Floor: R	Walls: R	Ceiling: R
	Rockwool/ Ceiling		Cellulose/Ceiling

2.f. Electrical

Service Load:	200 Amps		100 Amps
GFCI-Outlets in wet areas:	Yes		No
House wiring gauge (Romex):	10-2	12-2	14-2
Exterior outlets:	Yes	Where?	No
Electrical outlets attached to studs:	Yes		No
Striker plates in walls:	Yes		No
Clothes dryer vent in utility room:	Yes		No

2.g. Plumbing

Main lines:	CPVC	Polybutylene	Quest Pack
Hookup lines:	Flexible		Solid
Main shutoff valve:	Yes	Where:	No
Shutoff valves under sinks:	Brass	Plastic	None
Shutoff valves at toilets:	Yes		None
Plumbing access panels:	Yes		None
Outdoor spigots:	Yes	Where	None

2.h. Appliances

Furnace:	Electric	Gas	Manufacturer
Water heater:	Electric	Gas	Manufacturer
Air conditioner:	Capacity BTU's		Manufacturer
Stove:	Electric	Gas	Manufacturer
Refrigerator:	Over-under	Side-by-side	Manufacturer
	Capacity	Comments:	
Dishwasher:	Yes	No	Comments:
Other appliances:			
Available warranties:			
Cabinets:	Solid wood	Laminate	Solid wood facia only
Depth from wall:	Inches		

Table 3. Set-Up Checklist

	Home is placed properly
	Moisture barrier is securely placed on the ground
	Piers are set and straight
	Tie-downs are attached and tight
	Leveling of home is exact—was done with water leveling
	Sections (double, triple or quadruple-wides) are properly jointed
	Siding on ends (double, triple or quadruple-wides) is installed and looks unblemished
	Siding on front and rear (all models) is unblemished
	Steps and/or decks are in place and properly attached
	Fresh water lines are hooked up
	Waste water lines are hooked up
	Electricity is hooked up and working throughout the home
	Exterior trim is unblemished
	Roofing materials appear undamaged
	Outdoor lighting fixtures are attached and functioning
	All electrical switches and receptacles are working properly
	Gas lines (if necessary) are hooked up and not leaking
	All doors open and close properly
	All keys are accounted for and working properly
	All windows open and close properly—no cracks in glass
	Drapes, blinds, and valances are in place
	All plumbing fixtures work and don't leak
	All plumbing access panels have been located
	All water shutoff valves have been located

Setup Checklist, continued

	Plumbing joints have been hand tightened
	All appliances work properly
	All appliance paperwork is together, including warranties
	Interior walls have no cracks or blemishes
	Interior trim has no flaws
	Cabinet doors and drawers open and close flawlessly and with ease
	Stone masonry (if applicable) is not cracked and or loose
	Fireplace(s) is (are) in perfect working order
	Smoke detectors are in place and working properly
	Carpet has no flaws
	Vinyl flooring (or other) has no flaws
	Heat/AC registers are in place and working properly
	Outside AC exchange unit is installed and working properly
	Skirting is installed properly — neat and straight
	HUD tag is in place at rear of home (red tag)
	Furniture has arrived as ordered and is in perfect shape
	All other products have arrived and all services have been provided
	Dealer service rep and phone#
	Factory rep and phone#

Index

A